MOLIÈRE,
OR THE CABAL
OF HYPOCRITES
AND
DON QUIXOTE

The Cherry Orchard
The Inspector
A Month in the Country
The Seagull

MOLIÈRE, OR THE CABAL OF HYPOCRITES

AND

DON QUIXOTE

Two Plays by

MIKHAIL BULGAKOV

Translated from the Russian by
Richard Nelson, Richard Pevear
and Larissa Volokhonsky

THEATRE COMMUNICATIONS GROUP
NEW YORK
2017

Molière, or The Cabal of Hypocrites and *Don Quixote* are published by Theatre Communications Group, Inc., 520 Eighth Avenue, 24th Floor, New York, NY 10018-4156

The publication of *Molière, or The Cabal of Hypocrites* and *Don Quixote* by Richard Nelson, Richard Pevear and Larissa Volokhonsky, through TCG's Book Program, is made possible in part by the New York State Council on the Arts with the support of Governor Andrew Cuomo and the New York State Legislature.

TCG books are exclusively distributed to the book trade by Consortium Book Sales and Distribution.

Library of Congress Control Numbers:
2016046512 (print) / 2016048213 (ebook)
ISBN 978-1-55936-537-6 (trade paper) / ISBN 978-1-55936-861-2 (ebook)
A catalog record for this book is available from the Library of Congress.

Book design and composition by Lisa Govan
Cover design by John Gall

First Edition, June 2017

CONTENTS

INTRODUCTION

For English readers, the author of *The Master and Margarita* needs no introduction. The novel, which was first published in Russian in 1966–1967, twenty-six years after Mikhail Bulgakov's death, appeared at once in two English translations, both of which are still in print, and it has acquired four more over the past fifty years. Bulgakov wrote two other novels: *The White Guard* in 1923–1924 and *Theatrical Novel* (also known as *Black Snow*, though the author himself called it *Notes of a Dead Man*) in 1936. The first two parts of *The White Guard* were published in the magazine *Rossiya* in 1925, but the magazine was quashed before the third part could appear, and the book itself came out only in 1966; *Theatrical Novel* was not published until 1965. Bulgakov began the first version of *The Master and Margarita* (called *The Engineer's Hoof*) as early as 1928, went back to it repeatedly during the last decade of his life, and dictated the final revisions just three weeks before his death on March 10, 1940, at the age of forty-nine. He believed that it would some day be published, but he had no idea when. He entrusted it to fate.

The strange publishing history of these three novels, which are among the finest works of twentieth-century Russian literature, testifies to the enormous disorders, and the equally enormous "orders," that overtook Russia in the early twentieth century. If we first became aware of Mikhail Bulgakov as a novelist, however, in Russia his literary reputation during his lifetime and for many years after rested chiefly on his work as a playwright and an all-around man of the theater. Bulgakov began work on *The White Guard* when he was thirty, but he had already been bitten by the theater as a young boy in his native Kiev. "For Bulgakov," writes Anatoly Smeliansky, "the theater was to remain a place full of the naive magic and mystery, the colors and smells which were an inalienable part of the provincial theater of his youth."* As he himself put it, he had the stage in his blood.

Bulgakov's parents belonged to the Russian intelligentsia. His father, Afanasy Ivanovich Bulgakov, an essayist and theologian, was a professor at the Kiev Theological Academy; his mother was a teacher. Their son remained loyal to those origins and, at considerable risk in revolutionary times, proudly defended what he called "the finest stratum in our country." In high school he became interested in literature, theater and opera, and during the summers he took part in amateur theatricals. However, on graduating in 1909 he enrolled in the medical school of Kiev University. In 1912 he wrote his first story ("You'll see, I'll become a writer," he said to his sister), but he also continued his medical studies. When the First World War broke out, he volunteered for the Red Cross and was sent to the front, where he was badly wounded. Later he was sent to work in various provincial hospitals, before he finally returned to Kiev in 1918 to start a private practice. But by then there had been the two Russian revolutions of 1917, followed by the Civil War, which continued in his region until 1921.

---

* Anatoly Smeliansky, *Is Comrade Bulgakov Dead?*, translated by Arch Tait (London: Methuen, 1993), 18. I am much indebted to this detailed account of Bulgakov's life in the theater by one of the directors of the Moscow Art Theatre and the rector of its School for Academic Studies.

This period was especially chaotic in Kiev and the Ukraine. There were many warring factions—the Red Army of the Bolsheviks, the anti-Bolshevik revolutionaries, the pro-imperial White Army, the Ukrainian nationalists under Symon Petlyura, the Ukrainian anarchists under Nestor Makhno, and foreign forces from several countries. Between 1918 and 1920 there were some fourteen coups d'état. In 1919 Bulgakov was recruited into Petlyura's forces. He escaped, only to be mobilized by the White Army and sent as a doctor to the far-off city of Vladikavkaz, in the foothills of the Caucasus near the Georgian border. There he decided to abandon medicine definitively and began to write for the local newspaper. He also wrote his first plays, three of which were staged in the city's theater between June 1920 and January 1921. In that same year he sent some of the plays to a competition held by the newly organized People's Commissariat of Education in Moscow. "I dream of Moscow and the best theaters in the country," he wrote to his sister. On September 27, 1921, he stopped dreaming and moved to Moscow, where, as he wrote, "I arrived with neither money nor luggage . . . and stayed for good."

At first Bulgakov found work in the literary section of the People's Commissariat of Education, but soon he started writing for several newspapers, publishing a great number of articles and sketches on a great variety of subjects, some of which were collected under the titles *Notes on the Cuff* and *Notes of a Young Doctor*. In 1925 he published his first book, a collection of five stories entitled *Diaboliad*. And by then he had also finished the final version of his novel *The White Guard*—an extraordinarily lucid depiction of the terrible events that overtook Kiev during the Civil War, as experienced by an intellectual family, the Turbins, and their close friends. He had already begun work on a dramatization of the same material, with no particular theater in mind, when, in April 1925, he received out of the blue a note from the director of the Moscow Art Theatre's Second Studio, inviting him to come and discuss matters of interest to both the theater and the author. The studio was seeking new plays for its next season; the director had read the two parts of *The White Guard* published in *Ros-*

siya and proposed that Bulgakov adapt the novel for the stage. On August 15, 1925, he presented the play to the assembled company of the Moscow Art Theatre. "It was the moment," writes Anatoly Smeliansky, "when the lifeline of a great Theater crossed with that of its new Author."[†]

Chekhov's *Seagull* became the symbol of the Moscow Art Theatre when it was founded by Konstantin Stanislavsky and Vladimir Nemirovich-Danchenko in 1898. Bulgakov's adaptation of his novel, re-titled *Days of the Turbins*, became the signal production of the post-revolutionary Moscow Art Theatre. It premiered on October 5, 1926, and had run to 987 performances by 1941, when it was interrupted by the war.

Bulgakov was immediately drawn into the collective life of the Moscow Art Theatre in his work on the adaptation, which involved collaborating not only with the actors of the younger Second Studio, but also with the two old masters of the theater, Stanislavsky and Nemirovich-Danchenko. Their work over the next year was intense, turbulent, at times confrontational; at one point Bulgakov even wrote a formal letter to the directors threatening to remove the play from production. Yet this was and remained the world and the work he had looked forward to from Vladikavkaz. During that same time he also saw his topical satire, *Zoyka's Apartment*, staged by the newly founded Vakhtangov Studio Theatre. The two plays premiered in October of 1926, the *Turbins* on the sixth, *Zoyka* on the twenty-eighth. Two years later, in December 1928, his play *The Crimson Island* opened at the Moscow Chamber Theater.

All three of these plays were warmly received by the public, but they were denounced by the ideological critics and theater functionaries of the time, who kept accusing Bulgakov of being a reactionary, an anti-revolutionary, a class enemy. Through their combined efforts in newspaper articles and behind closed doors, they finally managed, in 1929, to have the plays banned from the repertoires of all Soviet theaters. With his prose writings also banned, Bulgakov was left in a desperate situation. In September

[†] Smeliansky, 47.

he wrote to the government asking for permission to go abroad, but received no reply. In March of 1930 he wrote again. This letter was addressed to seven members of the Soviet government, including Stalin, whose copy was handed to him in person by the deputy director of the Bolshoi Theatre. It was a long and bold letter, ending with an extraordinarily direct appeal:

> I request the Soviet Government to take into account that I am not a political activist, but a writer, that I have given all the fruits of my labors to the Soviet stage . . .
>
> I ask it to be taken into account that for me not being allowed to write is tantamount to being buried alive.
>
> I appeal to the humanity of Soviet power and request that I, a writer who cannot be of use in his native land, be magnanimously permitted to leave.
>
> If what I have written is not convincing and I am condemned to a lifetime of silence in the USSR, I request the Soviet Government to give me work in my special field and find me a permanent post as a stage director in a theater . . . If I am not appointed a director, I ask to be given a permanent post as an extra. If I can't be an extra, I ask for a job as a stagehand.
>
> If this is impossible, I request the Soviet Government to do with me what it finds fit, but to do something, because I, a dramatist who has written five plays and is known in the USSR and abroad, am *at the present moment* faced with poverty, the street, and ruin.[‡]

This time Bulgakov received a reply. It came in the form of a phone call from Stalin himself. His wife Elena noted down the brief conversation afterwards:

[‡] Quoted in the article "Bulgakov's Fate: Fact and Fiction" (1966), written by Vladimir Lakshin, translated by K. M. Cook-Florujy (Moscow, Raduga Publishers, 1990).

STALIN: We have received your letter. And read it with the comrades. You will have a favorable answer to it. But perhaps we should let you go abroad, eh? Are you really so sick of us?

BULGAKOV: I have thought a great deal recently about whether a Russian writer can live outside his country, and it seems to me that he can't.

STALIN: You're right. That's what I think, too. Where do you want to work? In the Art Theatre?

BULGAKOV: Yes, I would like to. But I asked about it and was refused.

STALIN: Well, you send an application there. I think they will agree.

And so they did. Bulgakov was immediately issued a contract and remained affiliated with the Moscow Art Theatre as dramatist, adapter, director, and actor for much of the coming decade.

Many questions have been asked about Stalin's intentions regarding Bulgakov. Perhaps, as an absolute ruler, it suited him to be unpredictable, to keep everyone off balance, to arrest and execute some writers and be indulgent to others. He may also have been impressed by Bulgakov's directness. And while he had dismissed *The Crimson Island* as "waste paper," it seems he genuinely admired *Days of the Turbins*. In 1932, talking with the directors of the Art Theatre during an intermission, he asked why the play was no longer being staged, and it was quickly returned to the repertoire. Stalin had attended the opening performance and eventually saw the play some twenty times. "So it is hardly surprising," writes Vladimir Lakshin, that in his radio broadcast to the Soviet people on July 3, 1941 announcing the German invasion, "Stalin, searching for words which would go straight to the heart of each and everyone, consciously or unconsciously used the phraseology and intonation of Alexei Turbin's monologue on the staircase at the gymnasium: 'To you I turn, my friends . . .'"

. . .

The ambiguous relations between art and power are central to the two plays brought together here. Though one is about the long-past era of French classical theater and the other is an "adaptation" of an even older novel, Bulgakov filled them with the immediacy of his own world and its conflicts.

He began work on *The Cabal of Hypocrites* in 1929, a few months after his plays were banned. Molière's *Tartuffe* had also been banned, and Molière had had many other run-ins with the authorities. Yet *The Cabal* is not simply a disguised self-vindication on Bulgakov's part; it is rather a broadening of Bulgakov's own struggles into an exploration of the fate of an artist in his confrontation with the forces of his time—an absolute monarch and a censorious Church. The parallels are there, but the larger vision is there as well. *The Cabal* is also a play about the theater itself, the physical theater, the curtains, the wings, the dressing rooms, a stage within the stage, a cheering or hooting audience. It is, finally, a play about Molière acting out his life.

Bulgakov finished the first version of *The Cabal* in early 1930 and submitted it to the Art Theatre. After much discussion with members of the theater, the government's Chief Repertory Committee decided that it did not properly reflect the class struggle and was therefore unsuitable for performance. A year and a half later, the play was reconsidered by the same committee, this time with support from Maxim Gorky, and was approved, with the title changed to *Molière*. But the problems with the production did not end there.

The contract Bulgakov received from the Art Theatre stated, on instructions from Stanislavsky, that the play would be produced no later than May 1, 1933. Stanislavsky wanted meanwhile to stage Bulgakov's adaptation of Gogol's *Dead Souls*, the first work the writer undertook in his new position as a member of the Art Theatre. *Dead Souls* opened on November 28, 1932, was rather coolly received by the critics, but found its audience and remained in the theater's repertoire for several decades. Bulgakov was also busy with other things. He had started a new draft of *The Master and Margarita* the year before, and in the spring of 1932 he was commissioned to write a biography of Molière for the series "Lives of Remarkable People," founded and directed by Gorky. His *Life of Monsieur de Molière*, a "novelized biography" and one of his finest prose works, was submitted to the editors in 1933, but they found that it did not conform to the guidelines of the series. Bulgakov refused to alter it, with the result that it was published only thirty years later.

In March 1932, rehearsals for *Molière* had in fact begun, but the opening date kept being put off. Stanislavsky fell seriously ill in the spring of 1933, went abroad for treatment, and did not come back to Moscow until August 1934. The Art Theatre was also going through internal struggles between its older and younger members, which disrupted rehearsals. A new opening date was set for January 1935, and Stanislavsky himself took over the production, but disagreements between author and director delayed things again. In October, Nemirovich-Danchenko stepped in, and the play finally had its premiere on February 16, 1936. It was well received by the public, but the press was as hostile to Bulgakov as ever, and when a particularly harsh review entitled "External Glitter and False Content" appeared in *Pravda* on March 9, *Molière* was abruptly cancelled. There had been only seven performances.

In September 1936 Bulgakov resigned from the Art Theatre and went to work for the Bolshoi as a librettist and consultant. He had finished the first full version of *The Master and Margarita* in 1934, but kept making changes and additions. He had written several plays that had gone unproduced—*Flight* (1928), *Adam and Eve* (1931), *Bliss* (1934), *The Last Days* (1935), *Ivan Vasilyevich* (1935). In 1936 he began work on *Theatrical Novel*, a satirical rendering of his experiences in the Art Theatre. A year later he said in a letter to a friend: "My last attempts to write for the theaters were the purest quixotry on my part. I shall never repeat that . . ."§ But at the end of the same year, after turning down several other suggestions, he signed a contract with the Vakhtangov Theatre for a dramatization of—*Don Quixote!*

§ Smeliansky, 274.

Bulgakov obviously had to be very selective in the episodes and characters he took from the immense text of the *Quixote*, but his work was not only a matter of concentration and elimination. He also added material that is not in Cervantes. For instance, while the peasant girl Aldonza Lorenzo, who is transformed in Quixote's imagination into his beloved Dulcinea del Toboso, never actually appears in the novel, Bulgakov brings her on stage twice—at the beginning, when Quixote kneels to her and recites chivalric poetry, and at the end, when the "cured" Quixote acknowledges the prosaic truth. The love story of Quixote's niece Antonia and the scholar Sansón Carrasco in Act Three, Scene 5 and Act Four, Scene 9, a more mundane reality to balance the knight's ideal love for the inaccessible Dulcinea, is also Bulgakov's invention. The chatter of Maritornes, Palomeque, and the mule driver in Act Two, Scene 3 comes from Bulgakov, as does most of the scene with the Fierabras elixir. The slapstick play with masks in Act Three, Scene 5 is also pure Bulgakov, as is the dark and melancholy ending.

Bulgakov's additions to passages that *are* in Cervantes also speak for his intentions in dramatizing the novel. His Quixote sets out on his path more knowingly, as he explains to Sancho at the very beginning: "A poet and knight sings and loves not the one made of flesh and blood, but the one his tireless fantasy has created. I love her the way she appeared to me in my dreams. I love, O Sancho, my ideal!" The "poet" and his "ideal" are Bulgakov's words. When Sancho then dubs him the Knight of the Mournful Countenance, Quixote replies: ". . . the mournful knight has been born to turn our calamitous iron age into an age of gold!" And he calls Sancho to go with him: "We will fly through the world to take revenge on the fierce and strong for their offenses against the helpless and weak, to fight for insulted honor, to restore to the world what it has irretrievably lost—justice!" His idealism replaces the romantic and chivalric quests of Cervantes's "mad" knight. And his defeat at the end is the more profound and anguished. As he faces the disguised Sansón Carrasco in combat, he says to him:

But something suddenly frightens me much more than the point of your sword! It's your eyes! . . . Your gaze is cold and cruel, and I've suddenly begun to imagine that Dulcinea doesn't exist! No, she doesn't! . . . My brow is bathed in cold sweat at the thought! She doesn't exist! . . . But even so I won't utter the words you are trying to tear out of me. There is no woman more beautiful! But your heart of iron cannot understand that!

At the very end, he says to Sancho:

The damage done me by his steel is insignificant. Nor did he cripple my soul with his strokes. My fear is that he has cured my soul, and, having cured it, has taken it out of me without replacing it with another . . . He has deprived me of the most precious gift a man is endowed with—he has deprived me of my freedom!

Bulgakov started work on *Don Quixote* in December 1937. He interrupted it to make a sixth full revision of *The Master and Margarita*, which was finished in May 1938, and then went back to the play. The two works influenced each other by turns. Near the end of the play, the dying Quixote says to Sancho: "I want to look at the trees . . . See, the leaves are yellow . . . Yes, Sancho, the day is coming to an end, it's clear. I'm afraid, because I am meeting my sunset quite empty, and there's nothing to fill that emptiness." One of the last additions Bulgakov made to the novel, in 1939, was the opening of Chapter 32, *Forgiveness and Eternal Refuge*:

Gods, my gods! How sad the evening earth! How mysterious the mists over the swamps! He who has wandered in these mists, he who has suffered much before death, he who has flown over this earth bearing on himself too heavy a burden, knows it. The weary man knows it. And without regret he leaves the mists of the earth, its swamps and rivers, with a light heart he gives himself into the hands of death, knowing that she alone can bring him peace.

The two works, for all their differences, are both farewells. Doctor Bulgakov knew, before his fellow doctors officially diagnosed it, that he was suffering from hypertonic nephrosclerosis, the kidney disease that had taken his father's life in 1907.

Don Quixote was finished in September 1938 and approved for production by the Chief Repertory Committee in January 1939, but the author did not live to see it. On April 27, 1940, six weeks after his death, the play was given its first performance at the provincial Ostrovsky Drama Theater in Kineshma, and a year later it opened at the Pushkin Theater in Leningrad and the Vakhtangov Theatre in Moscow.

In the half century since Bulgakov's surprising reappearance, *Molière* has triumphed over the cabal of hypocrites and *Don Quixote* has regained his freedom in Russia and in theaters throughout the world.

—Richard Pevear

MOLIÈRE,

OR

THE CABAL OF HYPOCRITES

Rien ne manque à sa gloire,
Il manquait à la nôtre.

His glory lacks for nothing,
Ours was lacking him.

—*Inscription on the bust of Molière
installed in the Académie Française in 1778,
a century after the playwright's death.*

CHARACTERS

JEAN-BAPTISTE POQUELIN DE MOLIÈRE, famous playwright and actor

MADELEINE BÉJART, actress

ARMANDE BÉJART DE MOLIÈRE, actress

MARIETTE RIVALLE, actress

CHARLES VARLET DE LA GRANGE, actor, nicknamed "Recordbook"

ZACHARIE MOIRRON, actor famous for playing romantic leads

PHILIBERT DU CROISY, actor

JEAN-JACQUES BOUTON, candlesnuffer and Molière's servant

LOUIS LE GRAND (XIV), king of France

MARQUIS D'ORSIGNY, swordsman, nicknamed "One-eye" and "Lord-have-mercy"

MARQUIS DE CHARRON, archbishop of Paris

MARQUIS DE LESSAC, gambler

HONEST COBBLER, the king's buffoon

CHARLATAN with a harpsichord

UNKNOWN WOMAN in a mask

FATHER BARTHOLOMEW, wandering preacher

BROTHER FORCE AND BROTHER FIDELITY, members of the Cabal of the Holy Writ

RENÉE, Molière's decrepit nanny

NUN

PROMPTER

MEMBERS OF THE CABAL OF THE HOLY WRIT in masks and black
cloaks

COURTIERS, MUSKETEERS, etc.

The action takes place in Paris during the time of King Louis XIV.

ACT ONE

———

From behind the curtain comes the muffled laughter of a thousand people. The curtain opens. The set represents the theater of the Palais-Royal. Heavy curtains. A green poster with a coat of arms and ornaments. On it in big letters: "PLAYERS OF MONSIEUR . . ." and some smaller words. A mirror. An armchair. Costumes. By the curtain separating two dressing rooms, a harpsichord of enormous proportions. In the second dressing room, a very large crucifix, before which an oil lamp is burning. In the first dressing room, a door to the left, and a great many tallow candles (they evidently did not stint on light). On the table in the second dressing room, only a lantern with colored glass.

On decidedly everything, on objects, on people (except for La Grange), the stamp of an extraordinary event, of anxiety and agitation.

La Grange, not involved in the production, sits in his dressing room, deep in thought. He is wearing a dark cloak. He is young, handsome and solemn. The lamp throws a mysterious light on his face.

In the first dressing room, Bouton, with his back to us, is pressed to the parting in the curtain. And even by his back it can be seen that the performance arouses a feeling of avid curiosity in him. Charlatan sticks his mug through the door. Charlatan puts his hand to his ear—he listens. Laughter is heard, then a final burst of guffawing. Bouton seizes some ropes, and the sounds die out. A moment later Molière appears through the parting in the curtain and runs down the steps into the dressing room. Charlatan discreetly disappears.

Molière is wearing an exaggerated wig and a caricatured helmet. He is holding a broadsword. Molière is made-up as Sganarelle—a purple nose with a wart. Funny looking. Molière holds his left hand to his chest, like a man with a heart ailment. The greasepaint melts down his face.

MOLIÈRE
(Throws down the helmet, catches his breath) Water!

BOUTON
Here. *(Gives him a glass)*

MOLIÈRE
Phew! *(Drinks, listens with frightened eyes)*

The door bursts open. Du Croisy runs in, made-up as Punchinello, his eyes popping out.

DU CROISY
The king's applauding! *(Disappears)*

PROMPTER
(At the parting of the curtain) The king's applauding!

MOLIÈRE
(To Bouton) My towel! *(Wipes his forehead, nervous)*

8

MADELEINE

(Made-up, appears in the parting of the curtain) Quick! The king's applauding!

MOLIÈRE

(Nervously) Yes, yes, I hear. I'm coming. *(Crosses himself by the curtain)* Most pure Virgin, most pure Virgin. *(To Bouton)* Open up the whole stage!

Bouton first draws the curtain that separates the stage from us, then the immense one that separates the stage from the house. And now we see the stage in profile. It is higher than the dressing rooms and empty. The tallow candles in the chandeliers shine brightly. The house is not seen; all that is seen is a gilded loge at the edge, but it is empty. We only sense the mysterious, watchful blueness of the slightly darkened house. Charlatan's face appears momentarily in the doorway. Molière goes up to the stage, so that we see him in profile. He walks with a catlike gait to the footlights, as if stealthily, his neck bent, the feathers of his hat sweeping the floor. At his appearance, one unseen man in the house begins to applaud, after which there is thunderous clapping. Then silence.

Your . . . Majesty . . . Your Majesty. Most Serene Sovereign . . .

He speaks the first words with a slight stutter—in life he stutters a little—but then his speech smooths out, and with the first words it becomes clear that he is a first-rate actor. The wealth of his intonations, grimaces and movements is inexhaustible. His smile is infectious.

On behalf of the actors of Monsieur's company, your most faithful and most obedient servants, I thank you for the unheard-of honor you have done us by coming to our theater. And you see, Sire . . . words fail me . . .

Slight laughter flutters in the house and dies down.

Muse, my muse, O playful Thalia!
Every evening, heedful of your call,
By candlelight in the Palais-Royal, I . . . ah . . .
Put on my head the wig of Sganarelle.
Bowing, as is fit to do, quite low—
After all, it's thirty sous for the parterre—
To amuse Paris, O Sire, I must go
Pouring out stuff and nonsense everywhere.

Laughter runs through the house.

But tonight, O muse of comedy, I pray,
Come to my aid, come quickly, for you see
It's no small task, no small task, in a play
To get the Sun of France to laugh at me.

The house bursts into applause.

BOUTON

Ah, what a head! He thought up the sun.

CHARLATAN

(With envy) When did he write it?

BOUTON

(Haughtily) Never. Impromptu.

CHARLATAN

Is it possible?

BOUTON

Not for you.

MOLIÈRE

(Sharply changes tone:)
You bear the royal burden for us all.
I am a mere player—a trifling thing.

10

But I play in your time, and so stand tall,
Louis! . . .
   The great!! . . . *(Raises his voice)*
     French!! . . . *(Shouts)*
      King!! *(Throws his hat into the air)*

Something unimaginable starts happening in the house. A roar: "Long live the king!" The candle flames are blown flat. Bouton and Charlatan wave their hats, shout, but their voices are not heard. The broken calls of the royal guards' horns cut through the roaring. La Grange stands motionless by his light, having taken off his hat. The ovation ends, and silence ensues.

VOICE OF LOUIS
(Out of the blueness) I thank you, Monsieur de Molière.

MOLIÈRE
Your most obedient servants invite you to watch one more amusing interlude, if we're not boring you.

VOICE OF LOUIS
Oh, with pleasure, Monsieur de Molière.

MOLIÈRE
(Shouts) Curtain!

The main curtain conceals the house, and music immediately begins behind it. Bouton closes the curtain that separates the stage from us, and it disappears. Charlatan's face vanishes.

(Appears in the dressing room, muttering) The bastard! . . . I'll kill him! I'll cut his throat! . . .

BOUTON
Who does he want to kill in the hour of triumph?

11

MOLIÈRE

(Seizing Bouton by the throat) You!

BOUTON

(Shouts) I'm being strangled at the royal performance!

La Grange stirs by his light, but freezes again. At the shout, Madeleine and Rivalle come running in—Rivalle almost totally naked, she was changing. The two actresses grab Molière by the breeches, pulling him away from Bouton, while Molière kicks his feet at them. Molière is finally torn away with a piece of Bouton's caftan. They manage to throw Molière down in the armchair.

MADELEINE

You're out of your mind! The whole house can hear you!

MOLIÈRE

Let me go!

RIVALLE

Monsieur Molière! *(Covers Molière's mouth)*

The shocked Charlatan peeks through the door.

BOUTON

(Looking in the mirror, feels his torn caftan) Beautiful job . . . and quick, too. *(To Molière)* What's this about?

MOLIÈRE

This scoundrel . . . I don't understand why I keep the tormentor around. We've played it forty times, everything was fine, then the king comes and a candle falls from the chandelier, wax drips on the floorboards . . .

BOUTON

Maître, you yourself got up to your funny antics and knocked the candle over with your sword.

MOLIÈRE

Lies, you do-nothing!

La Grange buries his face in his hands and weeps softly.

RIVALLE

He's right. You swatted the candle with your sword.

MOLIÈRE

The audience laughs. The king's surprised . . .

BOUTON

The king's the most courteous man in France and didn't notice any candle.

MOLIÈRE

So I knocked it over? I did? Hm . . . In that case, why did I yell at you?

BOUTON

It's very difficult for me to say, sir.

MOLIÈRE

It seems I tore your caftan?

Bouton pretends to laugh.

RIVALLE

My God, look at me! *(Grabs a caftan and, covering herself with it, flies off)*

DU CROISY

(Appears in the parting of the curtain with a lantern) Madame Béjart, you're on, you're on, you're on . . . *(Vanishes)*

MADELEINE

Coming! *(Rushes out)*

MOLIÈRE

(To Bouton) Take this caftan.

BOUTON

Thank you.

He takes off his caftan and breeches and quickly starts putting on a pair of Molière's breeches with lace ruffles at the knees.

MOLIÈRE

Ehh ... And why the breeches?

BOUTON

Maître, you must agree, it would be the height of bad taste to combine such a wonderful caftan with these vile breeches. Kindly look: these breeches are a disgrace! *(Puts on the caftan as well)* Maître, I've discovered two silver coins of insignificant value in the pocket. How do you wish me to deal with them?

MOLIÈRE

How, indeed. I suppose, you crook, it would be best to put them in a museum. *(Corrects his makeup)*

BOUTON

I agree. I'll do that. *(Pockets the money)* Well, I'll go and trim the snuff. *(Arms himself with a candlesnuffer)*

MOLIÈRE

I beg you not to gawk at the king from the stage.

BOUTON

To whom are you saying that, maître? I, too, am courteous, seeing I'm French by birth.

14

MOLIÈRE

You're French by birth and a blockhead by profession.

BOUTON

You are a great actor by profession, and a boor by character. *(Disappears)*

MOLIÈRE

I committed some sin, and the Lord sent him to me in Limoges.

CHARLATAN

Monsieur director. Monsieur director.

MOLIÈRE

Ah, yes, you're here, too. I tell you what, sir . . . It's . . . Forgive me my candor—it's a second-rate trick. But the parterre public will like it. I'll put you on in the intermission during the week. By the way, how do you do it?

CHARLATAN

It's a secret, monsieur director.

MOLIÈRE

Well, I'll find out. Play a few chords, only softly.

Charlatan, smiling mysteriously, walks toward the harpsichord, sits on a stool some distance from it, and makes movements in the air as if he were playing. The keys of the harpsichord go down, producing a gentle music.

Damn!

He rushes to the harpsichord, tries to catch the invisible threads. Charlatan smiles mysteriously.

Well, all right. Here's an advance. There's a spring somewhere, right?

CHARLATAN
Will the harpsichord stay in the theater overnight?

MOLIÈRE
Of course. You're not going to lug it home with you.

Charlatan bows and exits.

DU CROISY
(Peeks in with a lantern and a book) Monsieur de Molière. *(Vanishes)*

MOLIÈRE
Yes. *(Vanishes, and immediately after he disappears a roar of laughter is heard)*

The door-curtain leading to the dressing room with the green lantern is drawn aside and Armande emerges. The features of her face are lovely and resemble Madeleine's. She is about seventeen years old. She wants to slip past La Grange.

LA GRANGE
Stop.

ARMANDE
Ah, it's you, dear Recordbook. Why are you hiding here like a mouse? I've been looking at the king. But I'm in a hurry.

LA GRANGE
You have time. He's onstage. Why do you call me "Recordbook"? Maybe I don't like the nickname.

ARMANDE
Dear Monsieur La Grange. The whole company respects you and your chronicle very much. But if you wish, I'll stop calling you that.

LA GRANGE
I've been waiting for you.

ARMANDE

Why?

LA GRANGE

Today is the seventeenth, and I've put a black cross here in the record book.

ARMANDE

Has something happened? Has somebody in the company died?

LA GRANGE

I've marked it as a bad, black evening. Give him up.

ARMANDE

Monsieur de La Grange, who gave you the right to interfere in my affairs?

LA GRANGE

Spiteful words. I implore you, do not marry him.

ARMANDE

Ah, so you're in love with me?

Muffled music is heard behind the curtain.

LA GRANGE

No, I don't like you.

ARMANDE

Let me pass, sir.

LA GRANGE

No. You have no right to marry him. You're so young. I appeal to what's best in you.

17

ARMANDE

The whole company's taken leave of its senses, I swear to God.
What business is it of yours?

LA GRANGE

I can't tell you, but it's a great sin.

ARMANDE

Ah, the gossip about my sister. I've heard. Nonsense. And even if
there was a romance between them, what is it to me? *(She tries to
push La Grange aside and pass by)*

LA GRANGE

Stop. Give him up! No? Well, then I'll kill you. *(Draws his sword)*

ARMANDE

You're a crazy murderer. I . . .

LA GRANGE

What drives you to disaster? You don't love him, you're a young
girl, and he . . .

ARMANDE

No, I do love him . . .

LA GRANGE

Give him up.

ARMANDE

I can't, Recordbook. We're lovers, and . . . *(Whispers in La Grange's
ear)*

LA GRANGE

(Sheathing his sword) Go, I won't keep you any longer.

ARMANDE

(Passing by) You're a violent man. You threatened me. I can't stand the sight of you anymore.

LA GRANGE

(Agitated) Forgive me, I wanted to save you. Forgive me. *(Wraps himself in his cloak and leaves, taking his lantern)*

ARMANDE

(In Molière's dressing room) Monstrous, monstrous ...

MOLIÈRE

(Appears) Ah!

ARMANDE

Maître, the whole world's up in arms against me!

He embraces her, and at that same moment Bouton appears.

MOLIÈRE

Ah, damn it all! *(To Bouton)* Tell you what: go and see to the candles in the parterre.

BOUTON

I've just come from there.

MOLIÈRE

Tell you what, then: go to the barmaid and bring me a carafe of wine.

BOUTON

I've already brought one. Here it is.

MOLIÈRE

(Softly) Tell you what, then: just get the hell out of here!

BOUTON

You should have said that in the first place. *(Sighs heavily, goes to the door)* Maître, tell me please, how old are you?

MOLIÈRE

What's that supposed to mean?

BOUTON

Some musketeers were asking me.

MOLIÈRE

Get out.

Bouton exits.

(Locking the door behind him) Kiss me.

ARMANDE

(Hangs on his neck) What a nose that is! You can't get under it.

Molière takes off the nose and wig and kisses Armande.

(Whispering to him) You know, I'm ... *(Whispers something in his ear)*

MOLIÈRE

My dear girl ... *(Reflects)* Now there's nothing to be afraid of. I've made up my mind. *(Leads her to the crucifix)* Swear that you love me.

ARMANDE

I love you, I love you, I love you ...

MOLIÈRE

You won't deceive me? Look, I already have wrinkles, I'm beginning to turn gray. I'm surrounded by enemies, and the disgrace would kill me ...

ARMANDE

No, no! How could I do that?

MOLIÈRE

I want to live another lifetime! With you! But don't worry, I'll pay for it, I'll pay! I'll create you! You'll be the leading actress, you'll become great. That's my dream, which means that's how it will be. But remember, if you don't keep your vow, you'll rob me of everything.

ARMANDE

I see no wrinkles on your face. You're so brave and so great, you can't have any wrinkles. You're—Jean . . .

MOLIÈRE

I'm—Baptiste . . .

ARMANDE

You're—Molière! *(Kisses him)*

MOLIÈRE

(Laughs, then speaks solemnly) Tomorrow you and I will be married. True, I'll have to endure a lot because of that . . .

A distant noise of clapping is heard. There is knocking on the door.

Ah, what a life!

The knocking is repeated.

We won't be able to meet at home, at Madeleine's, tonight. So here's what we'll do: when the theater lights are all out, come to the side door, in the garden, and wait for me. I'll bring you here. There's no moon.

The knocking turns into pounding.

BOUTON

(Shouts through the door) Maître ... maître ...

Molière opens the door. Enter Bouton, La Grange and One-eye in the uniform of the Company of Black Musketeers, with a black band over one eye.

ONE-EYE

Monsieur de Molière?

MOLIÈRE

Your most humble servant.

ONE-EYE

The king has ordered me to present you with his payment for a seat in the theater—thirty sous. *(He holds out the coins on a pillow. Molière kisses the coins)* But seeing that you labored for the king above and beyond the program, he has ordered me to make you an additional payment for the verses you composed and recited to the king— Here are five thousand livres. *(Hands him the money in a sack)*

MOLIÈRE

Oh, King! *(To La Grange)* Five hundred livres for me, the rest to be divided equally among the actors of the company and handed out to them.

LA GRANGE

I thank you on behalf of the actors. *(Takes the sack and exits)*

In the distance a triumphant guards' march soars up.

MOLIÈRE

Excuse me, sir, the king is leaving. *(Exits running)*

ONE-EYE

(To Armande) Mademoiselle, I'm very happy that chance . . . *(Coughs)* . . . has given me the occasion . . . Orsigny, captain of the Company of Black Musketeers.

ARMANDE

(Curtsying) Armande Béjart. Are you the famous swordsman who can run anybody through?

ONE-EYE

(Coughs) You, mademoiselle, are no doubt an actress in this company?

BOUTON

Here we go. Oh, my foolish maître!

ONE-EYE

(Looks in astonishment at the lace on Bouton's breeches) Did you say something to me, my esteemed fellow?

BOUTON

No, sir.

ONE-EYE

So you're in the habit of talking to yourself?

BOUTON

Precisely so, sir. You know, once upon a time I talked in my sleep.

ONE-EYE

You don't say.

BOUTON

Yes, by God. And—it's so curious, imagine . . .

ONE-EYE

What the hell is this! Lord-have-mercy ... *(To Armande)* Your face, mademoiselle ...

BOUTON

(Insinuating himself between them) I shouted wildly in my sleep. Eight of the best doctors in Limoges treated me ...

ONE-EYE

And helped you, I hope?

BOUTON

No, sir. They gave me eight bleedings in three days, after which I went to bed and lay unable to move, taking Holy Communion every other minute.

ONE-EYE

(Exasperated) You're an original, my fine fellow. Lord-have-mercy. *(To Armande)* I flatter myself, mademoiselle ... Who is this man?

ARMANDE

Sir, he's the candlesnuffer—Jean-Jacques Bouton.

ONE-EYE

(With reproach) My dear fellow, I'll be delighted to hear about your shouting in your sleep some other time.

Molière enters.

I have the honor of taking my leave. I'll run and catch up with the king.

MOLIÈRE

All the best.

One-eye exits.

ARMANDE

(To Molière) Good-bye, maître.

MOLIÈRE

(Seeing her out) There's no moon. I'll be waiting. *(To Bouton)* Ask Madame Madeleine Béjart to come to me. Put out the lights and go home.

Bouton exits. Molière changes his clothes. Madeleine, without her makeup, enters.

Madeleine, there's a very important matter. *(Madeleine puts her hand to her heart, sits down)* I want to get married.

MADELEINE

(In a dead voice) To whom?

MOLIÈRE

To your sister.

MADELEINE

Tell me you're joking, I beg you.

MOLIÈRE

No, God forbid.

The lights in the theater begin to go out.

MADELEINE

And me?

MOLIÈRE

You know, Madeleine, we're joined by deep ties, we're true friends, but we haven't been lovers for a long time . . .

MADELEINE

Remember when you were in prison twenty years ago? Who brought you food?

MOLIÈRE

You.

MADELEINE

And who has looked after you for these twenty years?

MOLIÈRE

You, you.

MADELEINE

Nobody drives out the dog that's guarded the house all its life. But you, Molière, you can drive it out. You're a terrible man, Molière, I'm afraid of you.

MOLIÈRE

Don't torment me. I'm in the grip of passion.

MADELEINE

(Suddenly kneels down and crawls toward Molière) But? But still . . . change your mind, Molière. Let's pretend this conversation never happened. Hm? Let's go home. You'll light the candles, I'll come to you . . . You'll read me the third act of *Tartuffe*. Hm? *(Fawningly)* In my opinion, it's a work of genius . . . And if you're in need of advice, who will you go to, Molière? She's a little girl . . . You know, you've aged, Jean-Baptiste, your temples are gray . . . You like your hot water bottle. I'll make it nice for you . . . Picture it, a candle burning . . . We'll light a fire, and everything will be so good. And if, if you can't—oh, I know you . . . There's Rivalle . . . Not bad, is she? What a body! . . . Hm? I won't say a word . . .

MOLIÈRE

Think what you're saying. What role you're taking on. *(Wearily wipes his sweat)*

MADELEINE

(Getting up from her knees, beside herself) Anyone you like, only not Armande! Curse the day I brought her to Paris!

MOLIÈRE

Hush, Madeleine, hush, please. *(In a whisper)* I must marry her . . . It's too late . . . I'm obliged to. Understand?

MADELEINE

Ah, so that's it! My God, my God! *(Pause)* I won't fight anymore, I have no strength. I'll let you go. *(Pause)* I'm sorry for you, Molière.

MOLIÈRE

You won't deprive me of your friendship?

MADELEINE

Don't come near me, I beg you. *(Pause)* Well, so—I'll leave the company.

MOLIÈRE

Taking revenge?

MADELEINE

God knows I'm not. Today was my last performance. I'm tired . . . *(Smiles)* I'll start going to church . . .

MOLIÈRE

So you're adamant. The theater will give you a pension. You've earned it.

MADELEINE

Yes.

MOLIÈRE

When your distress subsides, I believe your feeling for me will return, and you'll want to see me again.

MADELEINE

No.

MOLIÈRE

You don't want to see Armande either?

MADELEINE

I will see Armande. Armande must know nothing. Understand? Nothing.

MOLIÈRE

Yes.

The lights have all been put out. He lights a lantern.

It's late, let's go, I'll take you home.

MADELEINE

No, thank you, there's no need. Let me sit here in your room for a few minutes . . .

MOLIÈRE

But you . . .

MADELEINE

I'll leave soon, don't worry. Go . . .

MOLIÈRE

(Wraps himself in his cloak) Good-bye. *(Exits)*

Madeleine sits by the oil lamp, thinking, muttering. The light of a lantern is seen through the curtain. La Grange enters.

LA GRANGE

(In a solemn voice) Who has stayed in the theater after the performance? Who's here? Is it you, Madame Béjart? So it happened, did it? I know.

MADELEINE

I'm thinking, Recordbook.

Pause.

LA GRANGE

And you couldn't bring yourself to tell him?

MADELEINE

It's too late. She lives with him and she's pregnant. I can't tell him now. Let me be the only unhappy one, not the three of us. *(Pause)* You're a true knight, Varlet, you're the only one I've told the secret to.

LA GRANGE

Madame Béjart, I'm proud of your trust in me. I tried to stop her, but I didn't succeed. No one will ever know. Come, I'll take you home.

MADELEINE

No, thank you, I want to be alone and think. *(Gets up)* Varlet, *(Smiles)* I've abandoned the stage today. Good-bye. *(Starts to leave)*

LA GRANGE

Can't I still take you home?

MADELEINE

No. Go on with your rounds. *(Vanishes)*

La Grange goes to the place where he was sitting at the beginning of the play. He sets down the lantern, which casts a green light on him, opens the book, talks and writes.

LA GRANGE

February 17th. The royal performance. In token of the honor, I draw a lily. After the performance, in the dark, I found Madame Madeleine Béjart in anguish. She is abandoning the stage . . . *(Sets down the pen)* The cause? A horrible event—Jean-Baptiste Poquelin de Molière, not knowing that Armande is not the sister but the daughter of Madame Madeleine Béjart, has married her, committing a mortal sin . . . That must not be written down, but as a token of the horror, I've drawn a black cross. And no one who comes after will ever suspect it. End of the 17th.

He takes his lantern and exits like a dark knight. For a time there is darkness and silence. Then, in the cracks of the harpsichord, light appears. There is a musical sound from the keys. The lid opens and Moirron climbs out, looking around thievishly. He is a boy of about fifteen with an extraordinarily handsome, depraved, and exhausted face. Ragged, dirty.

MOIRRON

They're gone. Gone. To hell with all of you, devils, demons . . . *(Whimpers)* I'm a miserable boy, dirty . . . haven't slept for two days . . . I never sleep . . . *(Sobs, puts his lantern down, collapses, falls asleep)*

Pause. Then the light of a lantern floats up, and Molière stealthily leads Armande in. She is wearing a dark cloak. Armande shrieks. Moirron instantly wakes up, terror on his face, trembling.

MOLIÈRE

(Threateningly) Speak up, who are you?

MOIRRON

Monsieur director, don't kill me, I'm Zacharie, the miserable Zacharie Moirron . . .

MOLIÈRE

(Bursting into laughter) So that's it! Ah, that damned charlatan . . .

Curtain.

ACT TWO

———

The king's reception room. A multitude of lights everywhere. A white stairway leading no one knows where. At a card table the Marquis de Lessac is playing cards with Louis. A crowd of courtiers, dressed with extraordinary magnificence, watches Lessac. Before him lies a heap of gold; gold coins are scattered on the carpet. Sweat streams down Lessac's face. Only Louis sits; the rest are standing. All are hatless. Louis wears the uniform of a white musketeer, a dashingly cocked hat with a feather, a military cross on his chest, golden spurs and a sword. Behind his chair stands One-eye, who directs the king's game. Beside them, a musketeer with a musket stands motionless, never taking his eyes off Louis.

LESSAC

Three jacks, three kings.

LOUIS

You don't say.

ONE-EYE

(Suddenly) Excuse me, Sire. Marked cards, Lord-have-mercy!

The courtiers freeze. Pause.

LOUIS

You came to play with me using marked cards?

LESSAC

Yes, Your Majesty. The impoverishment of my estate . . .

LOUIS

(To One-eye) Tell me, Marquis, according to the rules of cards, how should I act in such a strange case?

ONE-EYE

Sire, you should smash him in the face with a candlestick. That's the first thing . . .

LOUIS

What a disagreeable rule. *(Takes hold of a candlestick)* This candlestick weighs about fifteen pounds. I suppose they should have set out lighter ones.

ONE-EYE

Allow me.

LOUIS

No, don't trouble yourself. And the second, you were saying . . .

COURTIERS

(Bursting into a chorus) Curse the dog!

LOUIS

Ah! Excellent! Be so kind as to send for him. Where is he?

The courtiers rush in different directions. Voices: "The Cobbler! The king wants the Honest Cobbler!"

(To Lessac) Tell me, how is it done?

LESSAC

With the fingernail, Your Majesty. On the queen, for instance, I put little zeroes.

LOUIS

(With curiosity) And on the jacks?

LESSAC

X's, Sire.

LOUIS

Extremely interesting. And how does the law look upon these actions?

LESSAC

(Upon reflection) Negatively, Your Majesty.

LOUIS

(Compassionately) And what might be done to you for it?

LESSAC

(Upon reflection) I might be put in prison.

HONEST COBBLER

(Enters noisily) I'm coming, I'm running, I'm flying, I've arrived. Here I am. Greetings, Your Majesty. Great Monarch, what has happened? Who do I have to curse?

LOUIS

Honest Cobbler, this marquis here was playing with me using marked cards.

33

HONEST COBBLER

(Crushed, to Lessac) You . . . So you . . . You . . . Have you gone batty or something? Play like that in the marketplace and they'll push your face in. Did I give it to him good, Sire?

LOUIS

Thank you.

HONEST COBBLER

Can I have an apple?

LOUIS

Please help yourself. Marquis Lessac, gather up your winnings.

Lessac stuffs his pockets with gold.

HONEST COBBLER

(Upset) Your Majesty, that's really . . . no, you're joking . . .

LOUIS

(Into space) Duke, if it's no trouble for you, put the Marquis de Lessac in prison for a month. Give him a candle and a deck of cards—let him draw crosses and zeroes on them. Then send him—and his money—to his estate. *(To Lessac)* Put the place in order. And one more thing: don't play cards anymore; I have a feeling you won't be so lucky next time.

LESSAC

Oh, Sire . . .

Voice: "Guards!" Lessac is taken away.

HONEST COBBLER

Out he goes!!

ONE-EYE

S-s-scoundrel!

The valets start bustling about and a table, set for one, appears before Louis as if from nowhere.

CHARRON

(Emerging by the fireplace) Your Majesty, allow me to introduce to you the wandering preacher, Father Bartholomew.

LOUIS

(Starting to eat) I love all my subjects, including the wandering ones. Introduce him to me, Archbishop.

Strange singing is already heard outside the door. The door opens and Father Bartholomew appears. First of all, he is barefoot; second, he is disheveled, belted with a rope, and mad-eyed.

BARTHOLOMEW

(Dancing in, singing) We are mad for Christ!

Everyone is astonished except Louis. Brother Fidelity—sanctimonious physiognomy with a long nose, in a dark caftan—detaches himself from the crowd of courtiers and steals up to Charron.

ONE-EYE

(Looking at Father Bartholomew, softly) A spooky fellow, Lord-have-mercy!

BARTHOLOMEW

Most glorious king in the world. I've come to tell you that the Antichrist has appeared in your realm.

Stupefaction on the courtiers' faces.

The godless one, the poisonous worm gnawing at the foundation of your throne, bears the name of Jean-Baptiste Molière. Burn him on the public square, together with his godless work *Tartuffe*. All the faithful sons of the church demand it.

At the word "demand," Brother Fidelity clutches his head. Charron changes expression.

LOUIS

Demand? Of whom do they demand it?

BARTHOLOMEW

Of you, Sire.

LOUIS

Of me? Archbishop, they demand something of me.

CHARRON

Forgive them, Sire. Today he obviously lost his mind. And I didn't know. It's my fault.

LOUIS

(Into space) Duke, if it's no trouble, put Father Bartholomew in prison for three months.

BARTHOLOMEW

(Cries out) Because of the Antichrist I suffer!

Movement—and Father Bartholomew disappears as if he had never been there. Louis eats.

LOUIS

Archbishop, come here. I want to speak privately with you.

The whole crowd of courtiers backs away to the stairs. The muske-teer backs away, and Louis remains alone with Charron.

Is he mad?

CHARRON

(Firmly) Yes, Sire, he's mad, but in his heart he's a true servant of God.

LOUIS

Archbishop, do you find this Molière dangerous?

CHARRON

(Firmly) Sire, he is Satan.

LOUIS

Hm. So you share Bartholomew's opinion?

CHARRON

Yes, Sire, I share it. Hear me out, Sire. Your cloudless and victorious reign has not been darkened by anything, and will not be darkened by anything as long as you love.

LOUIS

Love whom?

CHARRON

God.

LOUIS

(Taking off his hat) I do love Him.

CHARRON

(Raising his hand) He—is there, you—are on earth, and there is no one else.

LOUIS

Right.

CHARRON

Sire, there are no limits to your power and there never will be, as long as the light of religion rests upon your realm.

LOUIS

I love religion.

CHARRON

Then, Sire, I, and the blessed Bartholomew along with me, beg you—defend it.

LOUIS

You find that he has insulted religion?

CHARRON

He has, Sire.

LOUIS

The impudent actor is talented. Very well, Archbishop, I'll defend it . . . But . . . *(Lowering his voice)* I'll try to reform him, he may still serve the glory of our reign. But if he commits one more impudence, I will punish him. *(Pause)* This . . . blessed fool of yours . . . does he love the king?

CHARRON

Yes, Sire.

LOUIS

Archbishop, let the monk out after three days, but bring it home to him that when one speaks with the king of France, one must not utter the word "demand."

CHARRON

May God bless you, Sire, and may He bring your punishing hand down upon the godless man.

Voice: "Your Majesty's servant, Monsieur de Molière."

LOUIS

Let him come in.

Molière enters, bows to Louis from a distance, and walks past the greatly attentive courtiers. He has aged very much, his face is ill, gray.

MOLIÈRE

Sire!

LOUIS

Monsieur de Molière, I am dining, do you have any objections?

MOLIÈRE

Oh, Sire!

LOUIS

Will you join me? *(Into space)* Chair. Place setting.

MOLIÈRE

(Turning pale) Your Majesty, I cannot accept this honor. Spare me.

A chair appears, and Molière sits on the edge of it.

LOUIS

What is your attitude towards chicken?

MOLIÈRE

My favorite dish, Sire. *(Pleadingly)* Allow me to stand.

LOUIS

Eat. How is my godson doing?

MOLIÈRE

To my great grief, Sire, the baby died.

LOUIS

What, the second one, too?

MOLIÈRE

My children do not live, Sire.

LOUIS

You mustn't lose heart.

MOLIÈRE

Your Majesty, there has been no occasion in France when someone has dined with you. I am uneasy.

LOUIS

France, Monsieur de Molière, is here before you in this chair. She is eating chicken and is not uneasy.

MOLIÈRE

Oh, Sire, you alone in all the world can say that.

LOUIS

Tell me, what will your talented pen present to the king in the nearest future?

MOLIÈRE

Sire . . . whatever may . . . contribute to . . . *(Nervous)*

LOUIS

Your writing is witty. But you should know that there are subjects which must be touched upon with prudence. And in your *Tartuffe*, you'll agree, you have been imprudent. The clergy deserve respect. My writer could not be a godless man, I hope?

MOLIÈRE

(Frightened) Heavens no . . . Your Majesty . . .

LOUIS

Firmly believing that in the future your work will follow the right path, I authorize you to perform your play *Tartuffe* at the Palais-Royal.

MOLIÈRE

(Gets into a strange state) I love you, King! *(In agitation)* Where is Archbishop de Charron? Do you hear? Do you hear?

Louis stands up. Voice: "The royal supper is over."

LOUIS

(To Molière) Tonight you will make my bed.

Molière snatches two candlesticks from the table and goes ahead. Behind him comes Louis, and it is as if a wind blows—everything gives way before him.

MOLIÈRE

(Calls out in monotone) Make way for the king, make way for the king! *(At the top of the stairs he calls into the void)* You see, Archbishop, you can't lay a finger on me! Make way for the king! *(Trumpets sound loudly from above)* Tartuffe is authorized! *(Vanishes along with Louis)*

The courtiers all vanish. Only Charron and Brother Fidelity are left onstage—two black figures.

CHARRON

(By the stairs) No. The king won't reform you. Almighty God, arm me and lead me after the godless one, so that I overtake him! *(Pause)* And he falls down these stairs! *(Pause)* Come here, Brother Fidelity.

Brother Fidelity goes to Charron.

Brother Fidelity, what's the matter with you? Sending me a madman? You assured me he would impress the sovereign.

BROTHER FIDELITY

Who knew he would utter the word "demand"?

CHARRON

Demand!

41

BROTHER FIDELITY

Demand!

Pause.

CHARRON

Have you found the woman?

BROTHER FIDELITY

Yes, Archbishop, everything's set. She sent a note, and she'll bring him.

CHARRON

Will he follow her?

BROTHER FIDELITY

The woman? Oh, you can be sure of it.

One-eye appears at the top of the stairs. Charron and Brother Fidelity disappear.

ONE-EYE

(Making merry by himself) The preacher went fishing for the Antichrist and caught . . . three months in prison. True God, Lord-have . . .

HONEST COBBLER

(Appears from under the stairs) Is that you, Lord-have-mercy?

ONE-EYE

Well, let's say it is. You can simply call me the Marquis d'Orsigny. What do you want?

HONEST COBBLER

There's a note for you.

ONE-EYE

From whom?

HONEST COBBLER

Who knows? I met her in the park, and she was wearing a mask.

ONE-EYE

(Reading the note) Hm . . . What sort of woman was she?

HONEST COBBLER

(Studying the note) Of easy morals, I think.

ONE-EYE

Why?

HONEST COBBLER

Because she writes notes.

ONE-EYE

Fool!

HONEST COBBLER

What are you name-calling for?

ONE-EYE

Is she well built?

HONEST COBBLER

That you'll find out for yourself.

ONE-EYE

Right you are. *(Exits pensively)*

The lights begin to fade, and dark musketeers, like phantoms, appear by the door. A voice from the top of the stairs drawls: "The king is asleep." Another voice in the distance: "The king is asleep!" A third from underground, mysteriously: "The king is asleep."

HONEST COBBLER

I'll sleep, too.

He lies down on the card table, wraps himself in a door curtain with coats of arms, so that only his monstrous boots stick out. The palace dissolves in darkness and disappears . . .

Molière's apartment appears. Daytime. The harpsichord is open. Moirron, a very handsome, magnificently dressed young man of about twenty-two, plays tenderly. Armande listens in an armchair, not taking her eyes off him. Moirron finishes the piece.

MOIRRON

What do you say about my playing, Little Mama?

ARMANDE

Monsieur Moirron, I've already asked you not to call me "Little Mama."

MOIRRON

First of all, madame, I am not Moirron, I am Monsieur de Moirron. So there. Ha, ha. Ho, ho.

ARMANDE

Did you get your title for sitting in the harpsichord?

MOIRRON

Let's forget the harpsichord. It is covered over with the dust of oblivion. That was a long time ago. Now I'm a famous actor, all Paris applauds me. Ha, ha. Ho, ho.

ARMANDE

And I advise you not to forget that you owe it all to my husband. He pulled you out of the harpsichord by your dirty ear.

MOIRRON

Not by the ear, but by my no less dirty feet. Father's a decent man, no question, but he's jealous as the devil, and he has a terrible nature.

ARMANDE

I must congratulate my husband. He adopted an insolent twerp.

MOIRRON

I'm a bit insolent, it's true . . . That's my nature . . . But as an actor . . . No actor in Paris can match me.

He is excessively cheerful, like a man who is asking for trouble.

ARMANDE

Ah, how cocky! And Molière?

MOIRRON

Well . . . that goes without saying . . . There are three: the maître and me . . .

ARMANDE

And who is the third?

MOIRRON

You, Mama. You, my famous actress. You're Psyche. *(Softly accompanies himself, declaims)* Through the spring forest . . . flies a God . . .

ARMANDE

(Without expression) Get away from me.

MOIRRON

(Embraces Armande with his left arm, with his right hand he accompanies himself) How slim her waist . . . Amor the hero . . .

ARMANDE

His quiver brings . . . he aims an arrow . . . *(Anxiously)* Where's Bouton?

MOIRRON

Don't worry, the faithful servant went to the market.

ARMANDE

(Declaims) The goddess Venus love hath sent, / Come, lover, ere its heat is spent.

Moirron lifts the hem of her dress, kisses her leg. She trembles, closes her eyes.

Scoundrel! *(Anxiously)* Where's Renée?

MOIRRON

The old woman's in the kitchen. *(Kisses her other knee)* Let's go to my room, Mama.

ARMANDE

Not for anything, I swear by the most pure Virgin.

MOIRRON

Come with me.

ARMANDE

You're the most dangerous man in Paris. It was a bad hour, when we dug you out of the harpsichord.

MOIRRON

Come, Little Mama.

ARMANDE

No, I swear by the Virgin. *(Gets up)* I won't go.

She goes, disappears through the door with Moirron. Moirron locks the door with a key.

Why did you lock the door? *(Without expression)* You'll ruin me . . .

Pause.

BOUTON

(Enters with a basket of vegetables, carrot greens sticking out, sets the basket on the floor, listens) Strange. *(Takes his boots off, sneaks up to the door, listens)* Ah, the villain . . . But, ladies and gentlemen, I have nothing to do with it . . . I saw nothing, I heard nothing, I know nothing . . . Good Lord, he's coming! *(Vanishes, leaving the basket and his boots on the floor)*

Molière enters, sets down his stick and hat, and looks perplexedly at the boots.

MOLIÈRE

Armande!

The key turns instantly in the lock. Molière rushes through the door. Armande cries out from behind the door, there is a scuffle, then Moirron comes running out, holding his wig in his hand.

MOIRRON

How dare you?!

MOLIÈRE

(Running out after him) You bastard! *(Gasping for breath)* I don't believe it, I don't believe my eyes . . . *(Sinks into the armchair. The key turns in the lock)*

ARMANDE

(Behind the door) Jean-Baptiste, get a hold of yourself!

47

Bouton peeks through the door, retreats.

MOLIÈRE

(Shaking his fist at the door) So you eat my bread and for that you dishonor me?

MOIRRON

How dare you strike me! Watch out! *(Grabs the hilt of his sword)*

MOLIÈRE

Let go of that sword, vermin!

MOIRRON

I challenge you!

MOLIÈRE

Me? *(Pause)* Out of my house!

MOIRRON

You're crazy, Father. A real Sganarelle.

MOLIÈRE

Disgraceful tramp. I warmed you in my heart, but I'll also fling you into the abyss. You'll act in fairground plays, Zacharie Moirron, from this hour on you're no part of the Palais-Royal company. Go!

MOIRRON

What? You're throwing me out of the company?

MOLIÈRE

Go away, my adopted thief.

ARMANDE

(Behind the door, desperately) Molière!

MOIRRON

(At a loss) Father, you imagined it, we were rehearsing *Psyché* . . . you don't know your own play . . . What are you ruining my life for?

MOLIÈRE

Go away, or I will stick this sword in you.

MOIRRON

So. *(Pause)* It would be extremely interesting to know who's going to play Don Juan? La Grange, maybe? Ho, ho. *(Pause)* But watch out, Monsieur de Molière, you may regret your madness. *(Pause)* I know your secret, Monsieur de Molière.

Molière laughs.

You've forgotten Madame Madeleine Béjart, have you? She's at death's door . . . She prays all the time . . . And meanwhile, monsieur, France does have a king.

MOLIÈRE

Despicable, lying milksop, what are you driveling about?

MOIRRON

Driveling? I'll go straight from here to the archbishop.

MOLIÈRE

(Laughs) Well, thanks for the betrayal. I know you now. But know this, that if my heart might have softened before those words, after them—never . . . Clear out, you pathetic fool.

MOIRRON

(From the doorway) Damned Sganarelle!

Molière grabs a pistol from the wall, and Moirron disappears.

MOLIÈRE

(Shakes the door, then talks through the keyhole) Streetwalker.

Armande sobs loudly behind the door.

Bouton!

BOUTON

(In his stocking feet) Here I am, sir.

MOLIÈRE

Pimp!

BOUTON

Sir . . .

MOLIÈRE

Why are these boots here?!

BOUTON

Sir, it's . . .

MOLIÈRE

You're lying, I can see from your eyes that you're lying!

BOUTON

Sir, in order to lie one has to say something. And I have not yet uttered a word. I took my boots off, because . . . See these nails? They're hobnailed boots, damn them . . . So, you see, my feet clomped, and they were rehearsing, so they locked the door on me . . .

ARMANDE

(Behind the door) Right!

MOLIÈRE

Why the vegetables?

BOUTON

The vegetables play no part. None at all. I brought them from the market. *(Puts his boots on)*

MOLIÈRE

Armande! *(Silence. He talks through the keyhole)* Do you want me to die, or what? I have a bad heart.

BOUTON

(Through the keyhole) Do you want him to die, or what? . . . He has a bad heart . . .

MOLIÈRE

Get out! *(Kicks the basket)*

Bouton disappears.

Armande! . . . *(Sits down on a low stool by the door)* Bear with me a little while, I'll set you free soon. I don't want to die alone, Armande.

Armande comes out with a tearstained face.

Can you swear to it?

ARMANDE

I swear.

MOLIÈRE

Say something.

ARMANDE

(Snuffling) Such a playwright, but at home, at home . . . I don't see how they get along together. How? What have you done? It'll be all over Paris. Why did you throw Moirron out?

MOLIÈRE

Yes, true. A terrible scandal! But, you know, he's a scoundrel, a little viper . . . oh, a depraved boy, depraved, and I fear for him. Really, in despair he'll start dragging himself all over Paris. And I hit him . . . oh, how unpleasant . . .

ARMANDE

Bring Moirron back, bring him back.

MOLIÈRE

Let him wander around for a day, and then I'll bring him back.

Curtain.

ACT THREE

A stone basement lit by a three-candle chandelier. In a niche a communion chalice gleams. There is a table covered with red flannel, on it a Bible and some manuscripts. At the table sit members of the Cabal of the Holy Writ in masks. In an armchair, apart, without a mask, sits Charron. The door opens, and two sinister-looking men in black lead in Moirron, blindfolded, his hands bound. They release his hands and remove the blindfold.

MOIRRON

Where have you brought me?

CHARRON

That makes no difference, my son. Now, repeat your denunciation before this gathering of honest brethren.

Moirron is silent.

BROTHER FORCE

Are you dumb?

MOIRRON

(Coughs) I . . . Holy Archbishop . . . I didn't hear clearly then, and . . . maybe I'd better not say anything.

CHARRON

It seems, my son, that this morning you slandered Monsieur Molière to me.

Moirron is silent.

BROTHER FORCE

Answer the archbishop, you elegant trash.

Silence.

CHARRON

It grieves me to see, my son, that you did slander him.

BROTHER FORCE

Lying's bad for you, my dear actor. You'll have to go to prison, pretty boy, where you'll spend a long time feeding bedbugs. And we'll proceed with the case anyway.

MOIRRON

(Hoarsely) I didn't slander him.

BROTHER FORCE

Don't prolong my agony: tell all.

Moirron is silent.

Ho there!

Through the door come two men even more unpleasant looking than those who brought Moirron.

(Looking at Moirron's shoes) Pretty shoes you've got, but there are even prettier ones. *(To the torturers)* Bring in the Spanish boot.

MOIRRON

No, don't. Several years ago, as a boy, I was sitting in the charlatan's harpsichord.

BROTHER FORCE

How did you wind up there?

MOIRRON

I played the keyboard from inside. It was a trick, as if the harpsichord was playing by itself.

BROTHER FORCE

And so.

MOIRRON

Inside the harpsichord ... No, I can't, Holy Father ... I was drunk this morning, I forget what I told you.

BROTHER FORCE

For the last time I ask you not to stop.

MOIRRON

And ... at night I heard a voice say that Monsieur de Molière ... had married ... not the sister ... of Madeleine Béjart, but her daughter ...

BROTHER FORCE

In other words, my dear heart, you want to say that Molière married his own daughter?

MOIRRON

I'm not saying that, Holy Father.

BROTHER FORCE

But I am. Don't you know that Molière lived for twenty years with Madame Madeleine Béjart? So whose voice was it?

MOIRRON

I guess I imagined it.

BROTHER FORCE

All right, whose voice did you imagine?

MARRON

The actor La Grange's.

CHARRON

That's enough, thank you, my friend. You have fulfilled your duty honorably. Don't torment yourself. Every faithful subject of the king and son of the Church should consider it an honor to denounce a crime that is known to him.

BROTHER FORCE

He's not so bad. I didn't like him at first, but now I see he's a good Catholic.

CHARRON

(To Moirron) You, my friend, will spend a day or two in a place where they will treat you well and feed you, and then you will go with me to the king.

Moirron is blindfolded, his hands are bound, and he is taken away.

BROTHER FIDELITY

So the king became godfather to a child of incest. Heh, heh.

CHARRON

Precisely, dear brothers. And we must not wish the man dead, for we are Christians, but we must try to reform the sinner by opening the king's eyes to him. A sinner sins for a long time and thinks that God has forgotten him. But the Lord remembers all. And society must be shown what Molière is, so that it turns away from him. For that, brothers, a stranger is about to appear, and I ask Brother Fidelity to speak with him, because the man knows my voice.

A knocking at the door. Charron pulls the hood over his face and disappears in semidarkness. Brother Fidelity goes to open the door. Unknown Woman appears, in a mask, leading One-eye by the arm. He is blindfolded.

ONE-EYE

Enchantress, when will you finally allow me to take off the scarf? You might just trust in my word. Lord-have-mercy, your apartment smells damp.

UNKNOWN WOMAN

One more little step, Marquis ... There ... Take it off. *(Hides)*

ONE-EYE

(Takes off the scarf, looks around) Ah! Lord-have-mercy!

He instantly snatches out his sword with his right hand and a pistol with his left, and stands with his back to the wall, displaying a great experience of life. Pause.

Some of you have sword points sticking out from under your cloaks. There may be enough of you to kill me, but I warn you that three of you will be taken out of this pit feet first. I'm Lord-have-mercy. Don't move. Where's the slut who lured me into this trap?

UNKNOWN WOMAN

(From the darkness) I'm here, Marquis, but I'm no slut.

BROTHER FORCE

No, Marquis, a lady . . .

BROTHER FIDELITY

We beg you to calm down, no one wants to attack you.

BROTHER FORCE

Put your pistol away, Marquis, it looks like a hollow eye, and spoils the conversation.

ONE-EYE

Where am I?

BROTHER FIDELITY

In the basement of a church.

ONE-EYE

I demand to be let out of here.

BROTHER FIDELITY

Any moment now the door will be opened.

ONE-EYE

In that case why have I been lured here, Lord-have-mercy? First of all—it's not a conspiracy against the king's life, is it?

BROTHER FIDELITY

God forgive you, Marquis. Here we are all ardent admirers of the king. You are at a secret meeting of the Cabal of the Holy Writ.

ONE-EYE

Bah! The Cabal! I didn't believe it existed. What does it need me for? *(Holsters the pistol)*

BROTHER FIDELITY

Sit down, Marquis, I beg you.

ONE-EYE

Thank you. *(Sits down)*

BROTHER FIDELITY

We grieve over you, Marquis.

MEMBERS OF THE CABAL

(In chorus) We grieve.

ONE-EYE

I don't like it when people grieve. Get down to business.

BROTHER FIDELITY

We wanted to warn you, Marquis, that they laugh at you at court.

ONE-EYE

That's a mistake. I'm known as "Lord-have-mercy."

BROTHER FIDELITY

Who in France doesn't know of your incomparable skill? That's why they whisper behind your back.

ONE-EYE

(Slapping the table with his sword) Name names!

The members of the Cabal cross themselves.

BROTHER FORCE

Why the noise, Marquis?

BROTHER FIDELITY

The whole court whispers.

ONE-EYE

Speak, or I'll lose my patience.

BROTHER FIDELITY

Tell me, do you know that most vile play by a certain Jean-Baptiste Molière called *Tartuffe*?

ONE-EYE

I don't frequent the Palais-Royal theater, but I've heard of it.

BROTHER FIDELITY

In that play the godless comedian has mocked religion and its servants.

ONE-EYE

Naughty boy!

BROTHER FIDELITY

But it is not only religion that Molière has insulted. Being a hater of the aristocracy, he has affronted it as well. Tell me, do you by any chance know the play *Don Juan*?

ONE-EYE

I've heard of that one, too. But what does Orsigny have to do with that carnival booth at the Palais-Royal?

BROTHER FIDELITY

We have absolutely precise information that the pen pusher was portraying you, Marquis, as his hero Don Juan.

ONE-EYE

(Sheathing his sword) What is this Don Juan?

BROTHER FORCE

A godless man, a scoundrel, a murderer, and, forgive me, Marquis, a seducer of women.

ONE-EYE

(With a changed expression) So. Thank you.

BROTHER FIDELITY

(Taking a manuscript from the table) Maybe you'd like to acquaint yourself with the materials?

ONE-EYE

No, thank you, I'm not interested. Tell me, among those present might there be someone who thinks there were grounds for portraying Orsigny in this foul guise?

BROTHER FIDELITY

Is there anybody, brothers?

Total denial among the members of the Cabal.

There is no such person. So, kindly see what motives led us to invite you to our secret meeting in this strange way. Here, Marquis, there are people of your own circle, and you yourself understand how disagreeable it is for us . . .

ONE-EYE

Perfectly. I thank you.

BROTHER FIDELITY

Much-esteemed Marquis, we trust that what has been said today will remain between us, and no one will know that we have troubled you.

ONE-EYE

Don't worry, sir. Where is the lady who brought me?

UNKNOWN WOMAN

(Steps forward) I'm here.

ONE-EYE

(Grimly) I offer you my apologies, madame.

UNKNOWN WOMAN

God will forgive you, Marquis, and I forgive you, too. Please come with me, and I'll take you back to where we met. Allow me to blindfold you again, because the esteemed society does not want anyone to see the way to their meeting place.

ONE-EYE

If it's really necessary.

One-eye's face is covered, and Unknown Woman leads him away. The door closes.

CHARRON

(Removing his hood and coming out of the darkness) I declare the meeting of the Cabal of the Holy Writ adjourned. Let us pray, brothers.

MEMBERS OF THE CABAL

(Rise and softly sing) Laudamus tibi, Domine, rex aeternae gloriae . . .

. . . An enormous cathedral filled with incense, mist and darkness. Little lights wander about. The archbishop's small confessional with lighted candles in it. Two dark figures walk by, a hoarse whisper is heard: "Have you seen Tartuffe?" "Have you seen Tartuffe?"—and they are gone.

Armande and La Grange appear, leading Madeleine under the arms. She is gray haired and sick.

MADELEINE

Thank you, Armande. Thank you, Varlet, my faithful friend.

An organ begins to play on high.

LA GRANGE

We'll wait for you here. That's the archbishop's confessional.

Madeleine crosses herself and, having knocked softly, enters the confessional. Armande and La Grange wrap themselves in dark cloaks, sit on a bench, and are swallowed by darkness.

CHARRON

(Emerges in the confessional) Approach, my daughter. Are you Madeleine Béjart?

The organ falls silent.

I have learned that you are one of the most devout daughters of the cathedral. You are dear to my heart, and I myself chose to hear your confession.

MADELEINE

What an honor for me, a sinner. *(Kisses Charron's hands)*

CHARRON

(Giving Madeleine his blessing and covering her head with a cloth) Are you ill, poor thing?

MADELEINE

I am, my archbishop.

CHARRON

(Compassionately) So you want to leave the world?

MADELEINE

I want to leave the world.

The organ on high.

CHARRON

What is your illness?

63

MADELEINE

The doctors say my blood has gone bad. I see the devil and I'm afraid of him.

CHARRON

Poor woman. How do you save yourself from the devil?

MADELEINE

I pray.

The organ falls silent again.

CHARRON

For that the Lord will raise you up and love you.

MADELEINE

He won't forget me?

CHARRON

No. What are your sins, tell me?

MADELEINE

I have been sinning all my life, Father. I was a great harlot, I lied, for many years I was an actress and seduced everyone.

CHARRON

Do you remember committing some especially grave sin?

MADELEINE

No, I don't, Archbishop.

CHARRON

(Sorrowfully) Foolish people! And so you come with a red-hot nail in your heart, and no one there will take it out. Never. Do you understand the meaning of the word "never"?

MADELEINE

(Having pondered) I understand. *(Frightened)* Oh, I'm afraid!

CHARRON

(Turning into the devil) You'll see fires, and amidst them . . .

MADELEINE

. . . a sentry paces, paces . . .

CHARRON

. . . and whispers . . . Why didn't you leave your sin behind, why did you bring it with you?

MADELEINE

And I'll wring my hands, I'll cry out to God.

The organ plays.

CHARRON

And the Lord will no longer hear you. And you will slump down in your chains, and your feet will plunge into the fire . . . And it will be so forever. Do you understand the meaning of "forever"?

MADELEINE

I'm afraid to. If I did, I'd die at once. *(Cries out weakly)* I understand! And if I leave it here?

CHARRON

You will hear the eternal singing.

On high a procession walks by with candles and children's voices sing. Then it all disappears.

MADELEINE

(Groping around with her hands, as if in darkness) Where are you, Holy Father?

CHARRON

(Toneless) I'm here ... here ... here ...

MADELEINE

I want to hear the eternal singing. *(Whispers passionately)* Long, long ago I lived with two men, with Molière and with another, and I conceived a daughter, Armande, and all my life I've been tormented, not knowing whose she was ...

CHARRON

Ah, poor thing ...

MADELEINE

I gave birth to her in the provinces, where I spent some time away from Molière. When she grew up, I brought her to Paris and passed her off as my sister. Then he, overcome with passion, became intimate with her, and I didn't tell him anything, so as not to make him miserable as well. On account of me, he committed a mortal sin. He may be living with his own daughter, and I've been thrown into hell. I want to fly up to the eternal singing.

CHARRON

And I, an archbishop, by the power vested in me, unbind you and set you free.

MADELEINE

(Weeping with rapture) Now I can fly?

The organ sings out powerfully.

CHARRON

(Weeping happy tears) Fly, fly!

The organ falls silent.

Is your daughter here? Call her in, I'll forgive her involuntary sin as well.

MADELEINE

(Coming out of the confessional) Armande, Armande, my sister, go in, the archbishop will give you his blessing. I'm happy ... happy ...

LA GRANGE

I'll help you into the carriage.

MADELEINE

And Armande?

LA GRANGE

I'll come back for her. *(Leads Madeleine into the darkness)*

Armande enters the confessional. Charron emerges, frightening in a horned miter, and rapidly crosses Armande several times with a reverse devil's cross. The organ drones powerfully.

CHARRON

Tell me, do you know who was with me just now?

ARMANDE

(Horrified, suddenly understands everything) No, no, she's my sister, my sister.

CHARRON

She's your mother. You're the daughter of Molière and Madeleine. I forgive you. But flee from him, flee from him today.

With a weak cry, Armande falls backward and remains motionless on the threshold of the confessional. Charron disappears. The organ plays soothingly.

LA GRANGE

(Returns in semidarkness, like a dark knight) Armande, are you sick?

. . . Daytime. The king's reception room. Louis, in a dark caftan embroidered with gold, is at the table. Before him is the dark and exhausted Charron. On the floor sits Honest Cobbler, mending a shoe.

CHARRON

She confirmed it to me at confession before she died—and then I did not even deem it necessary, Your Majesty, to interrogate the actor La Grange, so as not to make too much of this vile business. And I stopped the investigation. Molière has stained himself with a crime. However, judge as it pleases Your Majesty.

LOUIS

I thank you, my archbishop. You have acted correctly. I think the case is now clear. *(Rings, speaks into space)* Summon Monsieur de Molière, the director of the Palais-Royal theater, at once. Dismiss the guards, I will speak with him in private. *(To Charron)* Archbishop, send me this Moirron.

CHARRON

At once, Sire. *(Exits)*

HONEST COBBLER

A kingdom can't exist without informers, eh, Great Monarch?

LOUIS

Hold your tongue, buffoon, and mend your shoe. So you don't like informers?

HONEST COBBLER

What's there to like? Such scum, Your Majesty.

Moirron enters. His eyes are harassed; he is frightened and looks as if he slept without undressing. He is greatly impressed by Louis, whom he is obviously seeing close up for the first time.

LOUIS

(Politely) Zacharie Moirron?

MOIRRON

Yes, Your Majesty.

LOUIS

It was you who sat in the harpsichord?

MOIRRON

It was I, Sire.

LOUIS

Did Monsieur de Molière adopt you?

Moirron is silent.

I asked you a question.

MOIRRON

Yes.

LOUIS

He taught you the art of acting?

Moirron weeps.

I asked you a question.

MOIRRON

He did.

LOUIS

What motive guided you in writing a denunciation addressed to the king? It is written here: "wishing to serve justice."

MOIRRON

(Mechanically) Right, wishing . . .

LOUIS

Is it true that he struck you in the face?

MOIRRON

It's true.

LOUIS

What for?

MOIRRON

His wife was unfaithful to him with me.

LOUIS

So. That need not be reported at an interrogation. You might have said: for personal reasons. How old are you?

MOIRRON

Twenty-three.

LOUIS

I announce to you some favorable news. The investigation has confirmed your denunciation. What reward would you like to receive from the king? Would you like money?

MOIRRON

(Gives a start. Pause) Your Majesty, allow me to join the king's players at the Hôtel de Bourgogne.

LOUIS

No. Our information says that you are a weak actor. Impossible.

MOIRRON

Me—weak? . . . *(Naively)* The Théâtre du Marais, then?

LOUIS

No again.

MOIRRON

Then what am I to do? . . .

LOUIS

What do you want with this dubious profession of actor? You're a man unstained. If you wish, you'll be taken into the king's service, in the investigative police. Submit an application in the king's name. It will be approved. You may go.

Moirron leaves.

HONEST COBBLER

A Judas, a Judas! . . .

LOUIS

Buffoon . . . *(Rings)* Monsieur de Molière.

As soon as Moirron vanishes through the door, La Grange appears in another doorway, leads Molière in, and at once vanishes. Molière is a strange sight—collar askew, wig in disorder, sword hanging crooked, face leaden, hands shaking.

MOLIÈRE

Sire . . .

LOUIS

Why did you come with a companion, when you were asked to come alone?

MOLIÈRE

(Smiling fearfully) My faithful disciple, the actor La Grange . . . brought me. Please understand, I had pains in the heart, and I couldn't come alone . . . I hope I've done nothing to anger Your

Majesty? *(Pause)* Please . . . a misfortune has befallen me . . . forgive me the disorder of my dress . . . Madeleine Béjart passed away yesterday, and my wife, Armande, fled from the house at the same time . . . Abandoned everything . . . Her dresses, imagine . . . a chest of drawers . . . rings . . . and left a crazy note . . . *(Takes a scrap of paper from his pocket, smiles ingratiatingly)*

LOUIS

The holy archbishop was right. You are not only a filthy blasphemer in your plays, you are also a criminal, you are—godless.

Molière freezes.

I announce to you the decision in the case of your marriage: I forbid you to appear at court, I forbid you to perform *Tartuffe*. Only to keep your company from starving to death, I allow you to perform your funny comedies at the Palais-Royal, but nothing else . . . And from this day on, beware of reminding me of your existence! I withdraw the king's patronage.

MOLIÈRE

Your Majesty . . . this is a disaster . . . worse than the scaffold . . . *(Pause)* What for?!

LOUIS

For daring to ask me to stand as godfather to your child by your own daughter. For the shadow of a scandalous marriage cast upon my royal name.

MOLIÈRE

(Sinking into an armchair) Forgive me . . . I can't stand . . .

LOUIS

Leave. The audience is over. *(Exits)*

LA GRANGE

(Peeking through the door) Well?

MOLIÈRE

A carriage . . . Take me . . . Send for . . .

La Grange vanishes.

Madeleine, advise me . . . but she's dead . . . What's happening? . . .

HONEST COBBLER

(Sympathetically) So, what is it you've done? You don't believe in God, right? . . . Eh! You're really in a bad way . . . Have an apple.

MOLIÈRE

(Mechanically takes the apple) Thank you.

Charron enters and stops. Looks at Molière for a long time. His eyes glitter with satisfaction. At the sight of Charron, Molière begins to revive—before, he was lying face down on the table. He rises, his eyes light up.

Ah, Holy Father! Are you pleased? Is this for *Tartuffe?* I understand why you've rushed to the defense of religion. You caught on, my reverend sir. I don't dispute it. My friends once said to me: "One day you ought to portray some putrid monk." So I went and portrayed you. Because where could I find anyone more putrid than you!

CHARRON

I grieve for you, my son, because anyone who follows this path is sure to wind up on the gallows.

MOLIÈRE

Don't call me your son—I'm not the devil's son! *(Draws his sword)*

HONEST COBBLER
Why the name-calling?

CHARRON
(Eyes glittering) But you won't even make it to the gallows. *(Casts a sinister gaze around)*

One-eye comes from behind the door, holding a cane.

ONE-EYE
(Silently approaches Molière, steps on his foot) Monsieur, you pushed me and did not apologize. You are a boor.

MOLIÈRE
(Mechanically) Forgi . . . *(Tensely)* You pushed *me*.

ONE-EYE
You're a liar.

MOLIÈRE
How dare you? What do you want from me?!

LA GRANGE
(Enters just then, changes expression) Maître, get out, get out this minute! *(Nervously)* Marquis, Monsieur de Molière is unwell.

ONE-EYE
I found him with a sword in his hand. He's well enough. *(To Molière)* My name is Orsigny. You, my dear sir, are a scoundrel.

MOLIÈRE
I challenge you!

LA GRANGE
(In horror) Get out. This is "Lord-have-mercy."

CHARRON

Gentlemen, what are you doing . . . in the king's reception room
. . . ah . . .

MOLIÈRE

I challenge you!

ONE-EYE

That's it. I won't insult you further. *(Sinisterly enjoying himself)*
God be my judge, great king! Receive me, damp Bastille! *(To La
Grange)* You, sir, will be a witness. *(To Molière)* Give him instruc-
tions about your property. *(Draws his sword, tests the tip)* No
instructions? *(Cries in a low, drawn-out voice)* Lord-have-mercy!
(Makes a cross in the air with his sword)

CHARRON

Gentlemen, come to your senses . . . gentlemen . . . *(Lightly flies up
the stairs and watches the duel from there)*

LA GRANGE

It's plain murder!

HONEST COBBLER

Cutting each other up in the king's reception room!

*One-eye grabs Honest Cobbler by the scruff of the neck; he stops talk-
ing. One-eye falls upon Molière. Molière, warding him off, hides
behind the table. One-eye leaps on the table.*

LA GRANGE

Throw down your sword, master!

Molière throws down his sword, sinks to the floor.

ONE-EYE

Pick up your sword.

LA GRANGE
(To One-eye) You can't stab a man who has no sword in his hand!

ONE-EYE
And I won't. *(To Molière)* Pick up your sword, you low-down coward.

MOLIÈRE
Don't insult me and don't fight with me. There's something I don't understand . . . You see, I have a bad heart . . . and my wife has left me . . . Diamond rings scattered on the floor . . . she didn't even take any linen . . . It's bad . . .

ONE-EYE
What is all this?!

MOLIÈRE
I can't understand why you fell upon me. I've seen you only twice in my life. You brought money? . . . But that was long ago . . . I'm sick, please, don't touch me . . .

ONE-EYE
I'll kill you after your first performance. *(Sheathes his sword)*

MOLIÈRE
All right . . . all right . . . it doesn't matter . . .

Honest Cobbler suddenly tears from his place and disappears. La Grange picks Molière up from the floor, grabs his sword, and leads him out. One-eye gazes after them.

CHARRON
(Comes down the stairs with burning eyes. Pause) Why didn't you kill him?

ONE-EYE

What business is it of yours? He dropped his sword, Lord-have-mercy!

CHARRON

Imbecile!

ONE-EYE

What!!! Filthy cleric!

CHARRON

(Suddenly spits at One-eye) Tphoo!

One-eye is so astounded that he spits back at Charron. The two go on spitting at each other. The door opens. The agitated Honest Cobbler comes flying in, and after him comes Louis. The two quarrelers are so carried away that they do not immediately stop spitting. The four stare at each other dumbly for a while.

LOUIS

Excuse me for interrupting. *(Vanishes, closing the door behind him)*

Curtain.

ACT FOUR

Molière's apartment. Evening. Candles in the candlesticks, mysterious shadows on the walls. Disorder, manuscripts scattered around. Molière, in a nightcap, underwear and dressing gown, sits in an enormous armchair. In another sits Bouton. On a table, two swords and a pistol. On another, supper and wine, to which Bouton puts his lips from time to time.

La Grange, in a dark cloak, paces back and forth, half-humming, half-murmuring something. He is followed by a dark knight's shadow on the wall.

LA GRANGE

That harpsichord . . . that harpsichord . . .

MOLIÈRE

Stop it, La Grange. You had nothing to do with it. Fate has come to my house and taken everything from me.

BOUTON

The veritable truth. I, too, have a tragic fate. For example, I used to sell little pies in Limoges . . . Nobody buys these little pies, of course. I wanted to become an actor, and I ended up with you . . .

MOLIÈRE

Shut up, Bouton.

BOUTON

I'll shut up.

A bitter pause. Then a creaking of the staircase is heard, the door opens, and Moirron enters. He is wearing not a caftan but some dirty jacket. Shabby, unshaven, and half drunk, with a lantern in his hand. Those sitting in the room shield their eyes with their hands. When they recognize Moirron, La Grange snatches a pistol from the table. Molière hits La Grange's arm. La Grange fires and hits the ceiling. Moirron, not surprised in the least, listlessly looks at where the bullet struck. La Grange grabs objects at random, breaks a jug, falls upon Moirron, throws him to the ground, and begins to strangle him.

LA GRANGE

Hang me, king, hang me . . . *(Growls)* Judas . . .

MOLIÈRE

(With suffering) Bouton . . . Bouton . . . *(Together they drag La Grange off of Moirron. To La Grange)* You'll be the death of me, you . . . with your shooting and noise . . . What more do you want? To commit a murder in my apartment?

Pause.

LA GRANGE

You creature, Zacharie Moirron, do you know me?

Moirron nods affirmatively.

Wherever you go this night, expect death. You won't see another dawn.

La Grange wraps himself in his cloak and falls silent. Moirron nods affirmatively to him, kneels before Molière, and bows to the ground.

MOLIÈRE

What have you come for now, my boy? My crime has been discovered, what else can you fish around for in my house? What more will you write to the king? Or do you suspect that I'm not only incestuous, but also maybe a counterfeiter? Go, search the cupboards and drawers. I give you permission.

Moirron bows down for the second time.

Stop bowing and tell me what you want.

MOIRRON

My esteemed and most precious master, you think I've come to ask forgiveness? No. I've come to reassure you: by no later than midnight I will hang myself under your window, on account of the fact that my life cannot go on. Here's the rope. *(Takes a rope from his pocket)* And here's the note: "I am going to hell."

MOLIÈRE

(Bitterly) How reassuring!

BOUTON

(Takes a sip of wine) Yes, a most difficult case. A certain philosopher said . . .

MOLIÈRE

Shut up, Bouton.

BOUTON

I'll shut up.

MOIRRON

I've come to be near you for a while. And if I did stay alive, I wouldn't give Madame Molière a single glance.

MOLIÈRE

You wouldn't be able to give her a glance, my son, because she's gone, and I'm forever alone. I have an impetuous character; I'll do something first, and only think about it afterwards. And so now, having thought and become the wiser after all that's happened, I forgive you and restore you to my house. Come in.

Moirron weeps.

LA GRANGE

(Opening his cloak) You're not a man, master, you're not a man! You're a rag to wipe the floor with!

MOLIÈRE

(To La Grange) Insolent pup! Don't talk about what you don't understand! *(Pause. To Moirron)* Stand up, you'll wear holes in your trousers!

Pause. Moirron gets up. Pause.

Where's your caftan?

MOIRRON

I pawned it in a tavern.

MOLIÈRE

For how much?

Moirron waves his hand.

(Grumbles) That's swinishness—leaving satin caftans in taverns. *(To Bouton)* Buy back the caftan! *(To Moirron)* They say you went wandering around and even wandered into the king.

MOIRRON

(Beating himself on the chest) And the king said to me: Spy, spy . . . You're a bad actor, he says . . .

MOLIÈRE

Ah, the human heart! Ah, my friend, my king! The king's mistaken: you're a first-rate actor, and you're no good as a spy, your heart's not in it. The only thing I regret is that I won't have very long to act with you. They've set a one-eyed dog of a musketeer on me, my son. The king has withdrawn his patronage, and they'll kill me. I've got to flee.

MOIRRON

Master, as long as I'm alive, he's not going to kill you, believe me. You know what a swordsman I am.

LA GRANGE

(Sticks his ear out of his cloak) You're an astonishing swordsman, true. But, you vile vermin, before you get near "Lord-have-mercy," buy yourself a funeral service in the cathedral.

MOIRRON

I'll stab him in the back.

LA GRANGE

That's just like you.

MOIRRON

(To Molière) I'll never leave your side, at home, in the street, night and day. That's why I've come.

LA GRANGE

Like a spy.

MOLIÈRE

(To La Grange) Stuff your mouth with lace.

MOIRRON

Dear Recordbook, don't insult me. Why insult a man who has no right to answer you back? You shouldn't touch me, there's a stain on me. And don't attack me tonight. You'll kill me, they'll hang you, and the Cabal will put the sword to our defenseless maître.

MOLIÈRE

You've grown considerably wiser since you disappeared from home.

MOIRRON

(To La Grange) Bear in mind that the maître was declared godless for *Tartuffe*. I was there in the basement of the Cabal . . . He is outside the law, which means—expect anything.

MOLIÈRE

I know. *(Gives a start)* Did somebody knock?

MOIRRON

No. *(To La Grange)* Take the pistol and a lantern, we'll go and keep watch.

La Grange and Moirron take swords and a lantern and leave. Pause.

MOLIÈRE

A tyrant, a tyrant . . .

BOUTON

Who are you talking about, maître?

84

MOLIÈRE

About the king of France . . .

BOUTON

Quiet!

MOLIÈRE

About Louis the Great! A tyrant!

BOUTON

That's it. We're both hanged.

MOLIÈRE

Oh, Bouton, today I nearly died of fright. A golden idol, and the eyes, would you believe it, were emeralds. My hands were covered in cold sweat. Everything started swimming askew, sideways, and I knew only one thing—that it was crushing me! The idol!

BOUTON

Both hanged, and I'm one of them. Side by side in the square. You're hanging here, and I'm kitty-corner. The guiltlessly perished Jean-Jacques Bouton. Where am I? In heaven. I don't recognize the surroundings.

MOLIÈRE

All my life I've been licking his spurs and thinking just one thing: don't crush me. And all the same—he crushed me! Tyrant!

BOUTON

And the drum beats in the square. Who stuck his tongue out at the wrong moment? It'll hang down to his waist.

MOLIÈRE

What for? You see, this morning I ask him, What for? I don't understand . . . I say to him: Your Majesty, I really hate such acts, I protest, I am insulted, Your Majesty, please explain . . . Please . . .

Maybe I didn't flatter you enough? Maybe I didn't grovel enough?
. . . Your Majesty, where will you find another kiss-ass like Molière?
But what for, Bouton? For *Tartuffe*. For that I humiliated myself.
I thought I'd find an ally. And that I did! Don't humiliate yourself,
Bouton. I hate lawless tyranny!

BOUTON

They'll set up a monument to you, maître. A girl by a fountain and
water spurting from her mouth. You're a distinguished man . . .
just keep quiet . . . May his tongue wither . . . Why do you want to
ruin me?

MOLIÈRE

What more must I do to show I'm a worm? But you see, Your Majesty, I'm a writer, I think . . . and I protest, she's not my daughter.
(To Bouton) Ask Madeleine Béjart to come here, I want her advice.

BOUTON

What are you saying, maître?!

MOLIÈRE

Ah . . . she died . . . Why, old girl, didn't you tell me the whole
truth? . . . Or, no, why, why didn't you shape me, why didn't you
beat me . . . You see, she says, we'll light candles . . . I'll come to
you. *(In anguish)* The candles are burning, but she's not here . . .
I tore your caftan? . . . Here's money for the caftan.

BOUTON

(Tearfully) I'll call somebody. That was ten years ago, what are
you . . .

MOLIÈRE

Pack everything up. Tomorrow I'll play for the last time, and we'll
flee to England. How stupid. It's windy on the sea, it's a foreign
language, and generally it's not about England, it's about . . .

The door opens and the head of old Renée appears in it.

RENÉE

There's a nun come to see you.

MOLIÈRE

(Frightened) What's that? . . . What nun?

RENÉE

You yourself wanted to give her the theater costumes to launder.

MOLIÈRE

Pah, you old fool, Renée, how you frightened me! Eh! Costumes!
Tell her to come to the Palais-Royal tomorrow at the end of the
performance. Fool!

RENÉE

Me? It was you who ordered it.

MOLIÈRE

I ordered nothing.

Renée vanishes. Pause.

So, any other business? Ah, yes, the caftan . . . Show me, where
did I tear it?

BOUTON

Maître, go to bed, for God's sake. What caftan?

Molière suddenly gets under the blanket and pulls it up over his head.

Almighty God, make it so that nobody heard what he said. Let's
play a trick. *(In an unnaturally loud and false voice, as if continu-
ing a conversation)* So what are you saying, my dear sir? That our
king is the best, the most magnificent king in the whole world?
You'll get no objections from me. I share your opinion.

MOLIÈRE

(From under the blanket) Giftless nonentity!

BOUTON

Quiet! *(In a false voice)* Yes, I shouted before, I shout now, and I will always shout: Long live the king!

A knock on the window. Alarmed, Molière sticks his head out from under the blanket. Bouton cautiously opens the window, and the alarmed Moirron appears in it with a lantern.

MOIRRON

Who shouted? What's going on?

BOUTON

Nothing's going on. Why must something necessarily be going on? I was conversing with Monsieur de Molière and shouted: Long live the king! Doesn't Bouton have the right to shout something? So he shouted: Long live the king!

MOLIÈRE

God, what a giftless fool!

. . . *The actors' dressing rooms in the Palais-Royal. The old green poster hangs in the same place as before. There is the same green lantern in La Grange's room, and the oil lamp burns before the crucifix. But there is loud noise and whistling beyond the curtain. Molière sits in an armchair in a dressing gown and nightcap, made-up and with a caricature nose. Molière is excited, in a strange state, as if drunk. Next to him, in black doctor's clothes, but without makeup, stand La Grange and Du Croisy. Caricature doctor's masks are scattered about. The door opens and Bouton rushes in. At the beginning of the scene, Moirron stands at a distance, immobile, in a black cloak.*

MOLIÈRE

Well? Is he dead?

BOUTON

(To La Grange) The sword went . . .

MOLIÈRE

I ask that you address the director of the Palais-Royal, not the actors. I am still in charge at the last performance!

BOUTON

(To Molière) Yes, he's dead. The sword went through his heart.

MOLIÈRE

God rest his soul. Well, there's nothing to be done.

PROMPTER

(Peeking through the door) What's going on?

LA GRANGE

(Emphatically loud) What's going on? Musketeers broke into the theater and killed the doorkeeper.

PROMPTER

Ohh . . . My God . . . *(Vanishes)*

LA GRANGE

I, the secretary of the theater, announce: the theater is full of musketeers and unknown persons without tickets. I am powerless to control them, and I forbid the continuation of the performance.

MOLIÈRE

But . . . but . . . but! . . . He forbids! Don't forget who you are! You're a little boy compared to me. Look at my gray hair.

LA GRANGE

(Whispers to Bouton) Has he been drinking?

BOUTON

Not a drop.

MOLIÈRE

What else did I want to say?

BOUTON

My golden Monsieur de Molière . . .

MOLIÈRE

Bouton! . . .

BOUTON

. . . "Get out!" . . . I know. I've been with you for twenty years, and
all I've ever heard is that phrase, or "Shut up, Bouton"—and I'm
used to it. You love me, maître, and in the name of that love I beg
you on bended knee not to finish the performance, but to flee—the
carriage is waiting.

MOLIÈRE

What makes you think I love you? You're a babbler. Nobody loves
me. Everybody torments me and annoys me, they all pursue me.
And the archbishop has issued an order not to bury me in the cemetery . . . so everybody will be within the pale, and I'll croak outside. Know, then, that I have no need of their cemetery, I spit on it.
All my life you've persecuted me, you're all my enemies.

DU CROISY

For the love of God, maître, we . . .

LA GRANGE

(To Bouton) How can he play in such a state, how can he play?

Whistling and loud noise beyond the curtain.

Hear that?

MOLIÈRE

It's carnival time. They've broken the chandeliers in the Palais-Royal more than once. The parterre is making merry.

BOUTON

(Sinisterly) One-eye is in the theater.

Pause.

MOLIÈRE

(Growing quiet) Ah . . . *(Frightened)* Where's Moirron?

He rushes to Moirron and hides in his cloak. Moirron, his teeth bared, says nothing, embraces Molière.

DU CROISY

(In a whisper) We should send for a doctor.

MOLIÈRE

(Peeking from the cloak, timidly) He can't touch me onstage, can he? . . .

Silence. The door opens and Rivalle runs in. She is wearing a peculiar costume, is half naked as usual, on her head a doctor's hat, wheel-like spectacles.

RIVALLE

We can't drag out the intermission anymore . . . Either play or . . .

LA GRANGE

He wants to play, there's nothing we can do.

RIVALLE

(Looks at Molière for a long time) Play.

MOLIÈRE

(Emerging from the cloak) Good for you. Come, my brave old girl, I'll kiss you. How can we start the last performance and not finish it? She understands. You've been acting with me for twelve years, and, would you believe it, I've never once seen you dressed. You're always naked.

RIVALLE

(Kisses him) Eh, Jean-Baptiste, the king will forgive you.

MOLIÈRE

(Vaguely) He ... yes ...

RIVALLE

Will you listen to me?

MOLIÈRE

(After reflecting) I will. But not to them. *(Makes an awkward movement with his leg)* They're fools. *(Suddenly gives a start and changes abruptly)* Forgive me, gentlemen, I allowed myself to be rude. I myself don't understand how it escaped me. I'm nervous. Put yourselves in my position. Monsieur Du Croisy ...

DU CROISY, LA GRANGE AND BOUTON

(In chorus) We're not angry.

RIVALLE

Right after your last line, we'll lower you through the trapdoor, hide you in my dressing room till morning, and at dawn you will leave Paris. Agreed? Let's begin, then.

MOLIÈRE

Yes. We'll play the last scene.

Du Croisy, La Grange and Moirron seize their masks and disappear. Molière embraces Rivalle and she disappears. Molière takes off his dressing gown. Bouton opens the curtain that separates us from the stage. On the stage there is an enormous bed, a white statue, a dark portrait on the wall, a bed table with a little bell. The chandeliers are shaded in green, which creates a cozy night light onstage. Candles are lit in a booth, Prompter appears in it. Beyond the main curtain there is the noise of the house. Every now and then a sinister whistle soars up. Molière, changing abruptly, flits onto the bed with extraordinary lightness, lies down, covers himself with a blanket.

(Whispers to Prompter) Begin!

A gong strikes, the house beyond the curtain falls silent. Merry, mysterious music begins to play. Molière snores to it. With a rustle, the enormous curtain opens. It feels as if the theater is overcrowded. In the gilded loge at the edge some vague faces loom up. There is a loud roll of the kettledrum, and from under the floor La Grange rises, with an incredible nose, wearing a black cap, and peers into Molière face.

(Waking up, terrified)
By night, and in my bedroom, too?
You devil! Kindly get you gone!

Music.

LA GRANGE
Why such an insolent to-do?
It's me, your therapist, Pourgon!

MOLIÈRE
(Sits up on the bed in fright)
Sorry. But who's that hiding there?! . . .

93

The portrait on the wall tears open, Du Croisy sticks himself out of it—a drunken mug with a red nose, a doctor's spectacles and cap.

Why, here's another, I'm glad to see!

DU CROISY

(In a drunken bass)
The ve-ne-ree-o-logical chair
Has sent me here as deputy!

MOLIÈRE
Am I dreaming? Can it be?! . . .

The statue falls to pieces, and Rivalle flies out of it.

What is this wild incident?

RIVALLE

Of the medical faculty
I am the permanent president.

"Ha, ha, ha" in the house. Out of the floor grows a monster—a doctor of unbelievable height.

MOLIÈRE
A doctor who goes up two stories! . . .
Servants! Help! *(Rings)* I'm seeing things!

The pillows on the bed explode, and at the head Moirron emerges.

MOIRRON

It is I, Doctor Diafoirus,
Thomas, the incomparable. Who rings?

The third curtain falls, the furthest one, and from behind it emerges a Chorus of Doctors and Apothecaries in ridiculous and strange masks.

MOLIÈRE

But to what is this honor due? . . .
It seems the hour is rather late . . .

RIVALLE

We have come to you with news!

CHORUS OF DOCTORS

(Bursts out)
To be a doctor is your fate!!

RIVALLE

Who's the one that cures his stomach?

MOLIÈRE

He who on heaps of rhubarb feasts!

RIVALLE

Bene, bene, bene, bene.

CHORUS OF DOCTORS

Novus doctor dignus est.

DU CROISY

And what about, say, syphilis? . . .

MOLIÈRE

A good eight years on mercury.

"Ha, ha, ha" in the house.

LA GRANGE

Bravo, bravo, bravo, bravo,
A remarkable reply!

RIVALLE

He is truly full of knowledge . . .

DU CROISY

It comes tripping off his tongue!

One-eye suddenly appears in the loge, sits on the edge, and freezes in a pose of expectation.

MOIRRON

And there in the celestial college . . .

CHORUS OF DOCTORS

The doctors he will sit among!!

MOLIÈRE

(Suddenly falls down comically) Bring me Madeleine! To advise me . . . Help!

"Ha, ha, ha" in the house.

Parterre, don't laugh . . . quick . . . quick . . . *(Lies still)*

Music plays a few moments longer, then breaks off. In response to the beating of the kettledrum, a spooky Nun emerges in Molière's dressing room.

NUN

(Nasally) Where's his costumes? *(Quickly gathers all Molière's costumes and disappears with them)*

Commotion on the stage.

LA GRANGE

(Taking off his mask, at the footlights) Ladies and gentlemen, Monsieur de Molière, who played the role of Argan, has collapsed . . . *(Nervously)* The performance cannot be finished.

Silence, then a cry from the loge: "Give us our money back!" Whistling, noise.

MOIRRON

(Taking off his mask) Who shouted about money? *(Draws his sword, tries the point)*

BOUTON

(Onstage, in a stifled voice) Who could have shouted it?

MOIRRON

(Pointing to the loge) You or you? *(Silence. To One-eye)* Filthy animal!

One-eye, drawing his sword, climbs onto the stage.

(Goes catlike to meet him) Come on, come on. Closer. *(As he passes Molière, he looks at him, then sticks his sword into the floor, turns and leaves the stage)*

Prompter, in his booth, suddenly bursts into tears. One-eye looks at Molière, sheathes his sword, and leaves the stage.

LA GRANGE

(To Bouton) Close the curtain, will you!

The Chorus comes out of its stupor, the Doctors and Apothecaries rush to Molière, surround him in a frightful crowd, and he disappears. Bouton finally closes the curtain, the audience beyond it roars. Bouton runs after the group carrying Molière away.

Ladies and gentlemen, help me! *(Speaks through an opening in the curtain)* Ladies and gentlemen, I beg you . . . go home . . . something terrible has happened . . .

RIVALLE

(At another opening) Ladies and gentlemen . . . I beg you . . . ladies and gentlemen . . .

The curtain billows up, the curious try to get on the stage.

DU CROISY

(At a third opening) Ladies and gentlemen . . . ladies and gentlemen . . .

LA GRANGE

Put out the lights!

Du Croisy puts out the lights, knocking the candles down with his sword. The noise in the house dies down a little.

RIVALLE

(At the opening) Put yourselves in our place, ladies and gentlemen . . . go home . . . the performance is over . . .

The last candle is put out, and the stage sinks into darkness. Everything vanishes. Light plays on the crucifix. The stage is open, dark and empty. Not far from Molière's mirror, a dark figure sits crouched. A lantern floats onto the stage and the dark La Grange enters.

LA GRANGE

(In a solemn and stern voice) Who's still here? Who is it?

BOUTON

It's me, Bouton.

LA GRANGE

Why don't you go to him?

BOUTON

I don't want to.

La Grange goes to his dressing room, sits down, lit by the green light, opens the book, speaks and writes.

LA GRANGE

"February 17th. There was a fourth performance of the play *The Imaginary Invalid*, written by Monsieur de Molière. At ten o'clock in the evening, Monsieur de Molière, while performing the role of Argan, collapsed onstage, and was taken from us at once, without a confession, by inexorable death." *(Pause)* As a token of it, I draw a very big black cross. *(Thinks)* What was the cause of this? What? What shall I write down? Was the king's disfavor the cause of it, or was it the black Cabal? . . . *(Thinks)* What was the cause? Fate. That's what I'll write down. *(Writes and fades into the darkness)*

CURTAIN

DON QUIXOTE

Characters from the Village

ALONSO QUIXANO, alias Don Quixote de la Mancha

ANTONIA, his niece

HOUSEKEEPER OF DON QUIXOTE

SANCHO PANZA, Don Quixote's squire

PERO PÉREZ, the village priest

NICHOLAS, barber

ALDONZA LORENZO, Quixote's Dulcinea del Toboso, a peasant girl

SANSÓN CARRASCO, scholar

LEFTY PALOMEQUE, innkeeper

Characters from the Adventures

MARITORNES, servant girl at the inn

MULE DRIVER

TENORIO HERNANDEZ and PEDRO MARTINEZ, guests at the inn

MARTINEZ'S SERVANT

WORKMAN at the inn

DUKE

DUCHESS

DUKE'S MAJORDOMO

DUKE'S CONFESSOR

DOCTOR AGUERO

DOÑA RODRIGUEZ, duenna at the Duke's court

DUKE'S PAGE

PIG FARMER

WOMAN

FIRST AND SECOND OLD MAN

FIRST AND SECOND MONK

FIRST AND SECOND SERVANT

HERDSMEN

DUKE'S SUITE

The action takes place in Spain at the end of the sixteenth century.

ACT ONE

Scene 1

A summer evening. Don Quixote's yard, with stables, a well, a bench and two gates: one at the back of the stage, leading to the road; the other to the side, leading to the village. Also the interior of Don Quixote's house. In Don Quixote's room, a big bed under a canopy, an armchair, a table, an old suit of armor and a great many books. Nicholas appears in the yard with barber's paraphernalia.

NICHOLAS

Señora! Not here? *(Goes to the house, knocks)* Señor Quixano, may I come in? Señor Quixano! . . . Nobody's home. *(Goes into Don Quixote's room)* Niece! . . . Where is everyone? He said he wanted me to cut his hair! So—I'll wait. I'm in no hurry. *(Puts basin on the table, notices the suit of armor)* Look at that! Where'd he get all this stuff? Must be from the attic. What an odd bird! *(Sits down, takes a book from the table, reads)* The Mir-ror of Kni-ight-hood . . . Hm . . . I can't see what makes him love these knights!

QUIXOTE

(Offstage) Bernardo del Carpio! Bernardo del Carpio!

NICHOLAS

Is that him? It is. He's coming. *(Leans out the window)*

QUIXOTE

(Offstage) The great Bernardo del Carpio throttled the enchanted Roldan at Ronceval . . .

NICHOLAS

(At the window) What's this nonsense?

Quixote comes through the back gate with a book in one hand and a sword in the other.

QUIXOTE

Ah, if only I, the knight Don Quixote de la Mancha, in punishment for my mortal sins or in reward for the good I've done in my life, could finally meet the one I seek! Ah!

NICHOLAS

Who is this Don Quixote? Ehh, something's not quite right about him.

QUIXOTE

Yes, if it were granted me to meet my enemy—the giant Brandabar-baran in his snakeskin . . .

NICHOLAS

Brandabar . . . Has our hidalgo gone completely loony?!

QUIXOTE

. . . I'd follow Bernardo's example. I'd pick the giant up and throt-tle him in the air! *(Flings the book aside and begins slashing the air with his sword)*

NICHOLAS

Good God!

Quixote goes into the house. Nicholas hides behind the armor.

QUIXOTE

Is somebody here? Who's here?

NICHOLAS

It's me, Señor Quixano, sir, it's me . . .

QUIXOTE

Ah, at last fate has allowed me the happiness of meeting you, my mortal enemy! Come out here, don't hide in the shadows!

NICHOLAS

For God's sake, Señor Quixano, what are you talking about? What kind of enemy am I?

QUIXOTE

Don't pretend, your spells are powerless against me! I know you— you're the cunning magician Friston!

NICHOLAS

Señor Alonso, get ahold of yourself, I beg you! Look at me! I'm not a magician, I'm a barber, your good friend Nicholas!

QUIXOTE

You're lying!

NICHOLAS

For pity's sake! . . .

QUIXOTE

Come out and fight with me!

NICHOLAS

What am I going to do, he won't listen. Señor Alonso, come to your seses! This is a Christian soul before you, not a magician! Stop waving that sword around, señor!

QUIXOTE

Arm yourself and come out!

NICHOLAS

Dear God, help me! . . .

He jumps out of the window and runs off through the side gate. Don Quixote calms down, sits and opens his book. Someone walks by outside the fence. Strings twang, a heavy bass sings:

Oh, thy beauty, I opine,
Is brighter than a summer's day!
Where art thou, señora mine?
Or has all thought of me flown away?

Aldonza comes into the yard carrying a basket.

ALDONZA

Señora, señora! . . .

QUIXOTE

Whose voice do I hear? Is it the sorcerer confusing me again? . . . It's her!

ALDONZA

Señora, are you there?

She leaves her basket on the ground, goes to the house, knocks.

QUIXOTE

Is that her knocking? No, no, it's my heart pounding!

ALDONZA

(Goes in) Ah! Excuse me, señor, I didn't know you were here. It's me, Aldonza Lorenzo. Is your housekeeper here? I brought some salt pork and left it downstairs in the kitchen.

QUIXOTE

You have appeared just in time, señora. I am setting out to meet the giant Caraculiambro, the ruler of the island of Mamendrania. I mean to vanquish him and send him to you, so that he can fall on his knees before you and beg you to dispose of him as you wish . . .

ALDONZA

What on earth are you talking about?

QUIXOTE

I want him to tell you about his clash with Don Quixote de la Mancha . . . Know, O pitiless one, that this is Don Quixote before you!

ALDONZA

Señor Quixano, why are you kneeling?! I really don't know what to do . . .

QUIXOTE

Caraculiambro will tell you how it went. It was like this . . . *(Takes the book and starts reading)* "As soon as ruddy-cheeked Apollo scattered the threads of his golden hair over the earth, and golden-throned Aurora rose from the featherbed of her jealous husband . . ."

ALDONZA

Stop, señor, I beg you! I may be a simple girl, but still you shouldn't talk to me like this . . .

QUIXOTE

(Reads) "At that time Don Belianis mounted his steed and set out on his way . . ." *(Takes his sword)*

ALDONZA

I'm going to run and tell the housekeeper . . .

She disappears noiselessly.

QUIXOTE

I replace the name Belianis with the name Don Quixote . . . Don Quixote set out to meet danger and suffering, thinking only of you, my lady, O Dulcinea del Toboso! *(Looks around)* She's vanished! The bright ray is extinguished! Does it mean I was visited by a vision? Why, why, having beckoned, do you abandon me? Who has carried you off? Again I'm alone and dark magic clouds surround me. Away! I'm not afraid of you! *(Strikes the air with his sword, then calms down, sit and reads, muttering something . . .)*

Evening. A soft, mysterious whistling is heard outside the fence. The head of Sancho Panza appears above it. Sancho whistles again, then his head disappears. Sancho comes into the yard leading his gray donkey loaded with wineskins and bundles. He tethers the donkey, looks cautiously around, goes up the stairs and into Don Quixote's room, after whistling once more.

SANCHO

Sir . . .

QUIXOTE

Ah, it's you again, the indefatigable wizard! Well, you won't get away this time! Surrender!

SANCHO

(Going on his knees) I surrender.

Quixote puts the tip of his sword to Sancho's forehead.

QUIXOTE

At last you are in my power, contemptible sorcerer!

SANCHO

Señor! Open your eyes, before you stick that into mine! I surrender, I surrender twice, three times! I surrender definitively, irreversibly, once and for all. Take a good look at me, sinner that I am! What the hell kind of sorcerer am I? I'm Sancho Panza!

QUIXOTE

What's this? I know that voice. You're not lying? Is it really you, my friend?

SANCHO

Me, señor, me!

QUIXOTE

Why didn't you give me the prearranged signal?

SANCHO

I gave it, sir, three times, but the cursed magician stopped up your ears. I did whistle, sir!

QUIXOTE

You were within a hair's breadth of death! It's very good you decided to surrender. You acted like a wise man, Sancho, who understands that in desperate situations the bravest one saves himself for a better occasion.

SANCHO

I decided straight off that I had to surrender, as soon as you started poking that damned sword at my eyes!

QUIXOTE

You're right. But tell me, my friend, have you ever read anywhere of a knight possessed of greater valor than I?

SANCHO

No, sir, I haven't, because I can't read or write.

QUIXOTE

Well, sit down, and we'll make a final agreement about everything while nobody's here. So you accept my proposal to be my squire and to accompany me in my wanderings over the world?

SANCHO

I accept, señor, because I'm hoping you'll keep your promise and make me governor of the island you're going to conquer.

QUIXOTE

Never doubt what a knight tells you. Some squires have been made rulers of whole kingdoms for faithful service to their knights. And I hope to conquer such a kingdom in the nearest future. And since I have no need of it myself, I'll give it to you. You'll become a king, Sancho.

SANCHO

Hm . . . Let me think about that? . . .

QUIXOTE

What bothers you??

SANCHO

My wife, Juana Teresa. I'm afraid, Your Honor, that a queen's crown won't fit so well on her head. Better a simple governor's wife, and God knows if she can manage even that.

QUIXOTE

Rely on the will of Providence in all things, Sancho, and never demean yourself and wish for less than you're worth.

SANCHO

All the same there's no need to make me a king, governor's enough.

QUIXOTE

Splendid. Now we've agreed on everything, and it's just the time for us to leave secretly, while there's nobody home.

SANCHO

Good idea, sir, because your housekeeper . . . Frankly, she's the sort of woman . . . Well, let's just say, I fear her like the plague!

QUIXOTE

Help me into my armor.

Sancho helps him into his armor.

See what a helmet I've made for myself!

SANCHO

I'm a little worried, sir, that that might not be strong enough.

QUIXOTE

Oh, ye of little faith! Let's test it. Put it on, I'll give you the strongest blow I can, and you'll see what it's worth.

SANCHO

Yes, Your Honor.

He puts on the helmet. Don Quixote picks up his sword.

Wait, sir! I suddenly have this feeling that maybe we should first put it on the table to test it.

Sancho puts the helmet on the table.

QUIXOTE

Your cowardice makes me laugh. Watch!

He hits the helmet with his sword and smashes it to pieces.

SANCHO

Thank God my head wasn't in it!

QUIXOTE

Ah! . . . Ah! . . . What an irreparable misfortune. I can't set out without a helmet.

SANCHO

Señor, no helmet's better than with a helmet like that.

QUIXOTE

What are we going to do? Ah, I'm inconsolable . . . Ah, Sancho, look! *(Points to the barber's basin)* It's not for nothing they say that if fate closes one door before someone, another immediately opens. Oh, joy! The cowardly Friston forgot his helmet as he ran away!

SANCHO

Señor, that's a barber's basin, or I'm not my father's son!

QUIXOTE

Sorcery has blinded your eyes. Look and be convinced! *(Puts the basin on his head)* This is the helmet of the Saracen King Mambrino.

SANCHO

It looks just like a barber's basin.

QUIXOTE

What are you, blind?!

SANCHO

If you say so, Your Honor.

QUIXOTE

There, it's ready. He who stands before you is no longer the peaceful hidalgo Alonso Quixano, called the Good! I adopt a new name—Don Quixote de la Mancha!

SANCHO

Yes, sir!

QUIXOTE

And since a knight without a lady of his heart is like a tree without leaves, I choose as my lady the most beautiful woman in the world—the princess Dulcinea del Toboso. You probably knew her under the name of Aldonza Lorenzo.

SANCHO

Of course I knew her, señor. Only I wouldn't call her a princess, she's just a peasant. A very nice peasant, señor, and very strong, good looking. She could pull any knight out of the mud by his beard!

QUIXOTE

Stop, you insufferable babbler! Let Dulcinea be a peasant girl in your eyes and not a noble lady. What matters is that for me she is purer, better, and more beautiful than all princesses. Ah, Sancho, I love her, and that's enough for her to eclipse Diana! I love her, and that means in my eyes she is white as snow, her brow is the Elysian fields, her eyebrows are heavenly rainbows. Oh, my short-witted squire! A poet and knight sings and loves not the one made of flesh and blood, but the one his tireless fantasy has created. I love her the way she appeared to me in my dreams. I love, O Sancho, my ideal! Do you understand, do you understand me finally? Or do you not know the word "ideal"?

SANCHO

That's a word I don't know, but I hear you, señor. I see now that you're right, and I'm an ass. Yes, you're right, knight of the sad face.

QUIXOTE

What's that? What did you say?

SANCHO

I said "knight of the sad face." Don't be angry with me, sir.

QUIXOTE

Why did you say that?

SANCHO

I was looking at you just now in the moonlight, and you had the saddest face I've ever seen. Maybe you've worn yourself out in battle, or it's because you're missing several teeth on the right there and in the front. Who knocked them out, señor?

QUIXOTE

That is irrelevant! What is interesting is that winged wisdom put those words in your mouth unawares. And know that from this moment on that is what I shall call myself, and I shall have a sad face painted on my shield.

SANCHO

Why waste money on that, señor? All you have to do is uncover your face, and everyone will see right away who's standing before them.

QUIXOTE

Hah! There's a sharp man hidden behind that rather obtuse exterior! Well, then, let me be the Knight of the Sad Face, no, the Knight of the Mournful Countenance—I take the name with pride—but the mournful knight has been born to turn our calamitous iron age into an age of gold! I am to face dangers and woes, but also to perform great deeds! Let us go forth, Sancho, and resurrect the glorious Knights of the Round Table! We will fly through the world to take revenge on the fierce and strong for their offenses against the helpless and weak, to fight for insulted honor, to restore to the world what it has irretrievably lost—justice!

SANCHO

Ah, señor knight, if only that could happen! I've heard more than once that men who go to shear sheep often come back shorn themselves.

QUIXOTE

No, don't trouble my soul with your proverbs . . . I don't want to be torn by doubts. Let's hurry, Sancho, while the way is clear. *(They go out to the yard)* You'll now see my horse, he's not inferior to the Bucephalus that Alexander of Macedon rode on. *(Opens the stable door)* I call him Rocinante.

SANCHO

(Looking Rocinante over) Who was this Alexander of Macedon, sir?

QUIXOTE

I'll tell you about him on the way. Let's hurry. But what are you going to ride, may I ask?

SANCHO

My donkey, sir.

QUIXOTE

Hm . . . I've never read of squires riding donkeys.

SANCHO

A fine, sturdy donkey, sir . . .

QUIXOTE

Well, nothing to be done, let's go! Farewell, my dear, peaceful village, farewell! Forward, Sancho, the moon lights our path, and by morning we'll be far, far away. Forward!

SANCHO

Forward, ho!

Scene 2

A summer morning. A crossroads. To one side a forest, to the other a field. The wing of a windmill can be seen. Don Quixote and Sancho come onstage and stop.

QUIXOTE

We've come to a crossroads, Sancho. Here I'm sure we'll draw bucketsful from the lake of adventures.

He looks into the distance. Sancho dismounts from his donkey and tethers him by the roadside.

Fate has been kind to us. Look, look there, Sancho!

SANCHO

I don't see anything, señor.

QUIXOTE

Are you blind? Why aren't you amazed? Before us stands a row of giants with long, bony arms!

SANCHO

Señor, those are windmills!

QUIXOTE

How little you understand about knights' adventures. Those are wicked magician-giants, and we'll do battle with them at once! I'll exterminate their wicked breed!

The windmill begins to turn.

You won't frighten me, even if you have more arms than the giant
Briareus! Don't run away, vile creatures! Against you stands only
one knight, but he alone is worth all of you!

SANCHO
Get a hold of yourself, sir! What are you going to do?

QUIXOTE
Ah, fear has seized you! Well, then, stay here under the trees and
say your prayers! Forward, in the name of the beautiful and cruel
conqueror of my heart, Dulcinea!

He spurs Rocinante and rides off.

SANCHO
Stay here, señor! Where are you going, señor? *(Kneels)* Lord,
Lord, what is my master doing? Oh my God, he's attacking the
windmill with his lance! Señor!! Stop! That's it, he's been dragged
up! Dragged up! . . . Lord have mercy on us sinners!

*A heavy thud offstage. A barber's basin rolls onstage, followed by a
broken lance. Don Quixote enters, collapses, and lies there without
moving.*

I saw that coming! . . . God rest his soul! How quick our adventures
come to an end! Think, only yesterday evening we set off together
alive and well, full of hopes, and before I had time to hear the story
of Alexander of Macedon's amazing horse, my worthy master's
ribs are broken and he's gone to the next world! Ah, ah, ah!

*Takes a wineskin from his donkey, sits down beside Don Quixote,
drinks.*

How to get him home? I'll put him across the saddle . . . What
saddle? *(Looks into the distance)* The poor horse—lying there like

a sack of oats. I'll have to put him on my donkey. My poor friend, you've never borne such a sad burden.

Don Quixote moans.

Who's moaning? My master can't moan, he's dead. Maybe it's me moaning from grief? *(Drinks)*

QUIXOTE

(Weakly) Sancho . . .

SANCHO

What am I hearing? You're still alive, master?

QUIXOTE

Since you hear my voice, it means I'm still alive.

SANCHO

Thank Heaven, señor! I was about to heap you onto my gray donkey and bring you back to our village, to be buried there with the honors you deserve. You can't imagine how awful I felt, just thinking of the things your housekeeper was going to say to me! Take a sip . . . Ah, sir, sir, didn't I warn you those were windmills?

QUIXOTE

Never reason about what you don't understand, Sancho. And know that constant sorcery and magical transformations lie in wait for us. As soon as I pierced the arm of the first one with my lance, that cursed wizard, that same hateful Friston, turned all the giants into windmills, so as to deprive me of the sweetness of victory. Friston, Friston! How long will you pursue me with your hatred and envy? . . . Bring me my horse.

SANCHO

Not even Friston could manage that, señor. The poor beast isn't moving. Best to let him lie there and rest. If fate is willing, he may recover on his own; if not—the best we can do is skin him and sell his hide at the first market. Eh, sir!

QUIXOTE

Give me my lance.

SANCHO

The lance isn't good for much, Your Honor. *(Hands Don Quixote the pieces of the lance)*

QUIXOTE

This is a serious loss! What good is a knight without a lance? However, let us not grieve. You've read, of course . . .

SANCHO

Ah, sir, I already told you! . . .

QUIXOTE

Right, so you couldn't have read it.

SANCHO

No, sir, that I couldn't.

QUIXOTE

Well, I'll tell you, then, that the brave knight Don Diego Pérez de Vargas, having lost his weapons in battle, broke a huge branch from an oak, and on that same day killed so many Moors that their bodies lay stacked like firewood in the backyard.

SANCHO

What was his name again, sir?

QUIXOTE

Don Diego Pérez de Vargas. Bring me a heavy branch, Sancho.

SANCHO

Yes, sir. *(Leaves, comes back with a huge branch, and fixes the point on it)* Here's a new lance for you. I hope you slaughter no less Moors than this . . . Eh, I keep forgetting the name, but it's a beautiful name.

QUIXOTE

Don Diego Pérez de Vargas. He wasn't the only one who fought the Moors, Sancho. The valiant Rodrigo de Narvaez, alcalde of the fortress of Antequera, took the Moor Abindaraez prisoner at the very moment when he loosed his terrible battle cry, "Leliliez!"

SANCHO

You're quite a sight, sir.

QUIXOTE

Yes, my friend, I'm suffering great pain, and I don't complain only because knights are forbidden to complain.

SANCHO

If it's forbidden, then what can you do—but keep quiet. But for my money, let me tell you, sir, if something like that happened to me, you couldn't shut me up. Unless maybe that rule against complaining also applies to squires?

QUIXOTE

No, the rules of the order say nothing in that regard.

SANCHO

That's good.

QUIXOTE

Wait, wait! I see dust on the road. Yes, this is an incomparable place for adventures! But I must warn you, Sancho, much as you may be carried away by your fervor, you shouldn't take up the sword, whatever the danger I encounter, unless I'm attacked by people of your own estate.

SANCHO

You won't have to repeat that order twice, sir.

QUIXOTE

Look there! I was right. You see, two masked figures in black are coming, and far behind them a carriage. It's all clear: those two are magicians, and in the carriage is a princess they're abducting!

SANCHO

Maybe you should think that over a little, señor. Those are two monks, and servants behind them, and there aren't any magicians!

QUIXOTE

You're nearsighted, or else totally blind.

SANCHO

Sir, this could be even worse than the windmills!

QUIXOTE

Don't interfere with me! Your business is to observe the battle and then take charge of the rich booty we win.

Two monks appear.

Stop, you black devils!

Sancho hides behind a tree.

Stop! I demand that you immediately release the lady in the carriage! You've taken the poor woman captive by deceit!

FIRST MONK

What is this? I don't understand, sir! What lady? We're peaceful Benedictines going our way. That isn't our carriage . . . It turned off, it's headed a completely different direction.

QUIXOTE

I do not believe your deceitful words!

FIRST MONK

Sir, you are somehow strangely deluded . . .

QUIXOTE

Silence!

SANCHO

(From behind the tree) Silence!

QUIXOTE

Perfidious men, you shall taste the might of my sword! *(Draws his sword)*

FIRST MONK

Help! Servants! Help! Robbers! *(Runs off)*

SECOND MONK

Help!

QUIXOTE

(Pursuing First Monk) Stop, you vile spawn! You're mine, you're defeated!

Sancho whistles piercingly, leaps from behind the tree, rushes at Second Monk.

SANCHO

Leliliez! Surrender! You're mine!

SECOND MONK

(Falling to his knees) God save me!

SANCHO

Take your clothes off, you cursed Pérez de Vargas! *(Tears the hat and mask off Second Monk)*

SECOND MONK

Take everything, only leave me my life!

Gives his clothes to Sancho. Just then two servants come running in.

Save me! *(Runs off)*

FIRST SERVANT

What do you think you're doing, you damned highway robber?!

SECOND SERVANT

Thief!

SANCHO

Uh-uh-uh, back off, nice people. This doesn't concern you. This is my booty, fair's fair! We defeated the magicians, not you!

SECOND SERVANT

Ah, you big-mouthed bum!

FIRST SERVANT

Beat him!

The servants fall on Sancho with sticks.

SANCHO

Are you crazy? Help, señor! They're taking our booty!

FIRST SERVANT

Ah, you bastard!

SECOND SERVANT

Take that!

Second Servant grabs Sancho by the beard. The servants beat Sancho mercilessly.

SANCHO

Señor! . . . Señor! . . . Señor! . . . Leliliez! . . .

He falls down and doesn't move.

SECOND SERVANT

That'll teach you to go stripping innocent people!

The servants run off with the monk's clothing.

QUIXOTE

(Comes running in) The despicable fellow fled like a hare in a field! . . . What's the matter with you? God, he's dead!! What am I to do now? . . .

SANCHO

Ohh . . .

QUIXOTE

You're still alive?!

SANCHO

If you hear my voice—damn it—it means I'm still alive . . . If I ever again . . .

QUIXOTE

Ah, cursed memory! If I hadn't forgotten to prepare a vial of Fierabras elixir before we left, we'd have no fear of any wounds!

SANCHO

What elixir, sir?

QUIXOTE

It's a wonder-working medicine, Sancho. If you ever find me cut in two in battle—and that often happens with knights errant—don't be at a loss. Take the two halves, put them together as precisely as possible, and give me two sips of this elixir. You'll see me leap to my feet as fit and fresh as an apple. That's what kind of medicine it is, Sancho.

SANCHO

Sir, forget the governorship of an island, which you've promised me. Just give me the recipe for that elixir.

QUIXOTE

Don't worry, my friend, I'll tell you still more astonishing secrets, and make you prosperous for the rest of your life.

SANCHO

In that case, señor, I'm happy to accompany you . . . the pain even seems to be going away . . . *(Opens a bag, takes out food)* We'll need to fortify ourselves, sir. But then you won't want my simple food.

QUIXOTE

You have the wrong idea of knights, my friend. Knights dined well only at solemn banquets organized in their honor, but in ordinary times, that is, in the times of their errancy, they ate whatever came their way—most often, alas, flowers and dreams.

SANCHO

No flowers, sir, just bread, garlic, cheese, acorns. And the only dream I have now is to get my hands on the recipe of your elixir. Help yourself, sir.

QUIXOTE

You sit down, too. Why are you standing, my friend? What are you brooding about?

SANCHO

I'm thinking—you, a knight, are eating my simple food.

QUIXOTE

And I'm thinking about something else. You just said "my food." I'm thinking of the times when there were no such words as "mine" and "yours." When people, sitting peacefully as we're now sitting on the green grass, generously shared with each other what was sent them by benevolent nature, which never refused anything. What could people, tending their flocks, hide from each other? Transparent springs gave them water, trees gave them fruit. There was no gold, which generates lies, deceit, malice, and self-interest, and though there was none, that age, Sancho, is called the age of gold, and the dream of the knight errant, as I told you, is to revive that shining age! Ah, Sancho, if the troublesome happiness of being a knight errant hadn't fallen to my lot, I would have liked to be a shepherd. I'd be called Quixotis and you Pansino, and we'd wander over the hills and meadows, now singing love songs, now sighing from the bottom of our hearts. By day the luxuriant foliage of the oaks would shelter us from the burning sun; by night the peaceful stars would give us their light. Ah, don't you understand that only in such a life can man find true happiness, that that is his best lot?

SANCHO

You're an educated man, Your Honor, and you know tons of interesting things. You get talking, and a man can hang on your lips for hours at a time. But what is even more interesting is that elixir. Maybe you'll give me the recipe now? We don't want to forget about it during our adventures . . .

QUIXOTE

And I thought you were reflecting on the age of gold. Be patient: as soon as we reach some shelter, I'll prepare the elixir and reveal its secret to you.

Male voices are heard in the distance. Someone is whistling a tune.

Who's there?

SANCHO

(Peering off) Herdsmen, señor, from the Yanguas region. Daredevils, these Yangüeses, and a real band of brothers. I guess they're coming back from some fair.

Laughter is heard in the distance.

QUIXOTE

What are they laughing about?

SANCHO

One kicked your Rocinante. They're laughing at that, señor.

QUIXOTE

What's that you say? The brazen fellow dared to touch a knight's horse? I swear I won't rest until we've taught this company of scoundrels a good lesson!

SANCHO

For God's sake, sir, how are we going to do that? There's at least twenty of them, and just two—one and a half of us!

QUIXOTE

You forget that I alone am worth more than a hundred enemies!

Three herdsmen enter.

Be bold, Sancho, challenge them to answer you!

SANCHO

(To First Herdsman) Why did you kick another man's horse?

FIRST HERDSMAN

What horse are you talking about?

SANCHO

Don't be stupid!

SECOND HERDSMAN

Ah, that one? The one lying—legs up? We thought it was a skeleton, not a horse.

Fourth Herdsman enters.

QUIXOTE

You scoundrel, so you dare to laugh at the horse of the world's most famous knight?

SANCHO

Yes, you—scoundrel, answer me. You dare to do that?

SECOND HERDSMAN

Yes, I dare.

SANCHO

You do, eh?

HERDSMEN

Yes, we do!

Fifth Herdsman enters.

SANCHO

Take that, then! *(Gives Second Herdsman a box on the ear)*

SECOND HERDSMAN

And you take that! *(Gives Sancho a box on the ear)*

SANCHO

Help, señor!

Quixote strikes Third Herdsman with the side of his lance.

QUIXOTE
Defend yourselves, despicable riffraff!

THIRD HERDSMAN
Help me, boys!

FIRST HERDSMAN
Help, boys, they're beating our Yangüeses!

Sixth Herdsman and Seventh Herdsman run in.

FOURTH HERDSMAN
(Hitting Sancho) This way, brothers! They're beating up our Yangüeses!

FIFTH HERDSMAN
(Hitting Don Quixote) Come on, boys, don't let us down!

Sixth Herdsman falls upon Don Quixote, takes his lance away.

SIXTH HERDSMAN
Don't hang back, boys!

SEVENTH HERDSMAN
(Hitting Sancho) This way, boys! They want to beat us up!

Eighth Herdsman runs in.
    The herdsmen all fall upon Don Quixote, bring him down.

HERDSMEN
Don't let up, boys!

They beat Sancho.

SANCHO
(Trying to protect himself) Help, señor, we're getting beaten up!!

FOURTH HERDSMAN
Defend yourselves, brothers, they attacked us!

The herdsmen give Don Quixote and Sancho a bad beating. Ninth Herdsman, Tenth Herdsman and Eleventh Herdsman run in and fall upon Don Quixote and Sancho.

SANCHO
Save me!! I told you . . . I told you . . . Señor!!

QUIXOTE
(At his last gasp) Filthy scum! . . . Sancho, help me! . . .

SANCHO
Abindaraez . . . *(Lies still)*

TWELFTH HERDSMAN
(Runs in) Stop, what are you crazy? Stop! That's enough! We'll get in trouble! Look, they're not breathing!

FIRST HERDSMAN
Stop, what are you crazy, stop!

SECOND HERDSMAN
Enough, what are you crazy, stop!

HERDSMEN
Stop, what are you crazy, stop! Stop! . . .

FIRST HERDSMAN
Enough, boys. To hell with these bullies.

SECOND AND THIRD HERDSMEN

We got scared!

SECOND HERDSMAN

He hit me in the head! . . .

FIRST HERDSMAN

Damn it, we'll catch hell for this! Let's clear out of here, boys!

HERDSMEN

Let's clear out of here!

All the herdsmen leave. Don Quixote and Sancho are left lying in the grass without moving. The sad donkey stands nearby.
   Curtain.

ACT TWO

Scene 1

A summer evening. The inn of Lefty Palomeque. A well, a gate at the rear of the stage, an open shed with holes in the roof, two wings of the inn. From the windows of one comes loud laughter, the clink of glasses—a group of merry guests is having dinner. Maritornes is hanging laundry on a line.

MARITORNES

(Sings)
>Here doth a silent shepherd lie,
>His bloody breast without a breath.
>Why did the poor lad have to die?
>For love, for love he met his death . . .

MULE DRIVER

Greetings, my beauty!

MARITORNES

Ah! You should be ashamed of yourself, scaring people like that?
Hello.

MULE DRIVER

And hello to you, Maritornes! I haven't seen you for a long time.
I missed you. Look how pretty you are now!

MARITORNES

Oh, stop that!

MULE DRIVER

What am I doing, my dear Maritornes? Come here, I want to whisper something to you.

MARITORNES

Shame on you!

MULE DRIVER

I like that! How do you know what I want to whisper?

MARITORNES

We know what men whisper in girls' ears . . .
(Sings)
   Here doth a silent shepherd lie . . .

MULE DRIVER

Listen . . . I plan to spend the night here . . . so, when it's quiet . . .
come visit me . . .

MARITORNES

How dare you! Not for anything in the world! And where's the
landlord going to put you?

MULE DRIVER

I thought maybe—the shed.

PALOMEQUE

(From the wing) Maritornes! Maritornes!

MARITORNES

Get away from me! The landlord's calling!

PALOMEQUE

(Looking out the window) Maritornes! Where is that worthless girl?

MARITORNES

What do you want? I'm right here. Where else would I be?

PALOMEQUE

What are you doing?

MARITORNES

What do you think I'm doing? I'm hanging the laundry.

PALOMEQUE

Oh, "hanging the laundry" . . . We've got to keep an eye on you.

Mule Driver comes from behind the laundry.

MULE DRIVER

Landlord! Greetings. Good evening, Señor Lefty Palomeque!

PALOMEQUE

Ah, it's that kind of laundry! You are really something. Unbelievable! Turn my back for one second—and there's hanky-panky!

MULE DRIVER

No, landlord, don't scold her, she's a good girl. I just got here. We've barely said two words to each other.

PALOMEQUE

There are words and words. Two words can be worse than a whole long speech. We all know what she's like.

MARITORNES

It's not enough that family misfortunes force me to work at an inn for pennies . . .

PALOMEQUE

Well, well, enough, stop whimpering, you do-nothing.

Maritornes disappears.

What do you want?

MULE DRIVER

To spend the night.

PALOMEQUE

We've got a full house, there isn't a single bed . . . except in the shed . . . Want to sleep in the shed?

MULE DRIVER

In other words, with sky and stars for a blanket? The roof's nothing but holes.

PALOMEQUE

Ah, forgive me, esteemed señor! If I'd known you would grant us a visit, I'd have prepared a palace under a golden roof, with silk blankets. If you don't like it, go sleep in the field. I didn't invite you, we've got a full house, I told you.

MULE DRIVER

All right, all right, I'll take the shed.

PALOMEQUE

Here's a horse blanket! *(Throws it out the window)* Spread it out, you'll sleep like a king on a featherbed, everybody'll envy you.

Mule Driver takes the horse blanket and, passing by Maritornes, makes some mysterious signs.

MARITORNES

(Softly) Stop that, stop that! . . . *(Sings)*
Why this bloody wound so wide?
In his heart they thrust a knife,
And for love, for love he died . . .

HERNANDEZ

(In the window) Hey, landlord, more wine!

PALOMEQUE

Coming, señores!

He runs to the wing with a wineskin, then returns to his place. From the wing comes loud laughter and the twang of strings.

HERNANDEZ

(Sings)
Oh, Marquis of Mantua, Mantua, Mantua,
My uncle and my lord! . . .

Through the gate comes Sancho, bent double and leading his donkey by the bridle. Don Quixote, half alive, is riding on the donkey. Behind limps Rocinante, loaded with mangled armor and the makeshift lance. Sancho's head is bound in a rag, he has a black eye, half his beard is torn out.

SANCHO

Thank God we made it to an inn! Oh-h-h! . . . *(Sits on the edge of the well)* Hey, miss . . . miss . . . Come here!

MARITORNES

My oh my! There's a first time for everything!

SANCHO

(To Don Quixote) Wake up, señor, we're at an inn!

QUIXOTE

What?

SANCHO

Time to perk up, sir, you don't want them to take you for a sack of dung. We're at an inn.

QUIXOTE

What's that you say, Sancho? We're at a castle? Wait, a dwarf will come out now, blow on a trumpet, the drawbridge will be lowered, and we will enter . . .

SANCHO

What dwarfs? What bridges, señor? Come to your senses.

The sound of a swineherd's horn is heard.

QUIXOTE

Squire of little faith, do you hear the trumpet sounding? We're being met.

Groaning, Don Quixote dismounts from the donkey.

MARITORNES

What fun!

QUIXOTE

(To Maritornes) O beautiful señora! Allow me to introduce myself. I am the knight errant Don Quixote de la Mancha, known to fame as the Knight of the Mournful Countenance. I am that knight whose exploits have outshone the exploits of the Flaming Sword and Reinaldo de Montalbán, who carried off the golden idol of Mohammed! Your humble servant!

MARITORNES

Ah, many thanks, caballero. *(To Sancho)* He speaks so sweetly, so well, and yet so strangely. I don't understand a word.

MULE DRIVER

(Peeking out of the shed) What's this? Is that mangy rat making passes at Maritornes?

MARITORNES

(To Sancho) What is he, Greek or something?

SANCHO

Yes, Greek, he's a Greek, now can you arrange for us to spend the night, miss?

MARITORNES

Landlord, landlord!

PALOMEQUE

(Looking out the window) What do you want?

MARITORNES

Guests.

Palomeque, goggling his eyes, stares at Don Quixote, then comes out.

PALOMEQUE

What can I do for you?

QUIXOTE

Señor castellan, you see before you a knight who belongs to the order of knights errant and his squire.

PALOMEQUE

What are you talking about? . . . What "order"?!

QUIXOTE

We would be extremely grateful to you if you could give us shelter in your castle.

PALOMEQUE

Señor caballero, I can supply you with everything except a room and a bed—we don't have a single vacancy.

QUIXOTE

We'll be satisfied with little, for a knight's repose is battle, armor is his adornment, and the hard stones his bed.

MULE DRIVER

He really lays it on thick, the son-of-a-bitch!

PALOMEQUE

If that's the case, sir, you'll like my shed.

MULE DRIVER

What the hell are you doing, landlord, you gave me the shed.

PALOMEQUE

There's room enough for three. *(To Don Quixote)* How'd you end up looking like that, sir?

SANCHO

He fell off a cliff.

MARITORNES

What cliff? We've got no cliffs here.

SANCHO

I said he fell off a cliff, so that means there's a cliff somewhere.

PALOMEQUE

(To Sancho) And you, too, felt the urge to dive off this cliff?

SANCHO

Ahh, me too! That is, I didn't fall myself, but just seeing him fall made me ache all over.

MARITORNES

Oh, that does happen! I sometimes dream I'm falling, and when I wake up I'm aching all over.

PALOMEQUE

We know what you dream about, you don't need to tell us! Ho, there!

Workman runs in.

Take the horse and donkey to the stable.

QUIXOTE

I humbly beg you, señor castellan, to see that the horse is well looked after, because he's the best mount the world has ever seen.

MULE DRIVER

This one?

He makes a sign to Palomeque indicating that Don Quixote is out of his mind. Workman leads the donkey and Rocinante away.

SANCHO

(To Don Quixote) You should tell them about Alexander of Macedon, señor, otherwise they may not believe you. Let's go to the shed.

He leads Don Quixote to the shed. Everyone leaves the courtyard.

How much longer do you suppose, señor, before we're able to move our legs—to say nothing of—walking normal?

QUIXOTE

I admit that I am undoubtedly to blame for all that happened. In no case should I raise my sword against people who don't belong to the knightly estate. If we're ever attacked by a band like the one today, here's what we'll do: I won't even touch my sword, but you'll draw yours and cut them down without mercy. If knights come to their aid, only then will I step into it, and I'll be able to protect you. A good plan?

SANCHO

A very good one, señor, may lightning strike me! The thing is this, sir: I'm a peace-loving man, quiet, meek, calm, good natured, obliging—that's the first thing. The second thing, I don't have a sword, and I'm glad I don't. And, third thing, if I did, I wouldn't draw it, not against a simple man, against a nobleman, a peasant, a knight, a goatherd, a swineherd, a demon or a devil!

QUIXOTE

It's a pity that the pain makes it so hard to talk, otherwise I'd come up with a suitable objection. One thing I can tell you—with such a peace-loving character as yours, you ought to become the shepherd Pansino, but you'll never govern an island. You'd have enemies to deal with, and for that you need courage. Poor man! Understand that storms like we had today are inseparable from our occupation, which would lose all charm without them.

SANCHO

Just tell me one thing, señor: will harvests like the one we gathered today come one after another without a break, or will there be some space between them? If not, it seems to me, having gathered two, we might not be up to a third.

QUIXOTE

Forget the misfortune that befell us, Sancho. There's no remembrance that withstands time, no pain that's not cured by death. Right now we'll set about preparing the Fierabras elixir.

SANCHO

(Perking up) What's required for that, sir, tell me? Miss, hey, miss!

MARITORNES

What do you want?

SANCHO

It's this, my dear girl: we're about to prepare an elixir ...

MARITORNES

What sort of elixir?

SANCHO

A magic elixir, dear heart! Somebody gets cut in two in a battle, you see ... hop! ... give him a sip, and he's off again mowing down the Moors! ...

MARITORNES

Let me try some. I've got such heartaches, it's like a cat's clawing at it.

SANCHO

All right, we'll give you some. *(To Don Quixote)* So what's required, sir?

QUIXOTE

Take a big pot ...

SANCHO

(To Maritornes) You hear? A pot.

MARITORNES

A pot.

QUIXOTE

Pour five bottles of sweet red wine into it.

SANCHO

(To Maritornes) Got that?

MARITORNES

Got it.

QUIXOTE

Put in a handful of chopped garlic.

SANCHO

(To Maritornes) Remember that—a handful of garlic.

MULE DRIVER

(Enters) What're you making?

MARITORNES

They know this elixir . . . they're making an elixir . . . You get cut in two, you know . . .

MULE DRIVER

Ah, yes, yes!

QUIXOTE

Salt—four or five spoonfuls, big ones.

SANCHO

(To Maritornes) Are you listening?

MULE DRIVER

I know this. Four or five spoonfuls of salt. That's right.

MARITORNES

(Counting on her fingers) . . . Five.

QUIXOTE

A pinch of hot red pepper . . . a handful of chopped acorns, some vinegar, three bottles of lamp oil, and a teaspoon of oil of vitriol.

MULE DRIVER

That's exactly right. I know this elixir.

QUIXOTE

Mix it together well, and heat it up.

MARITORNES

Right. I'll go do it at once.

MULE DRIVER

I'll give you a hand. It's a good elixir, it even helps mules, especially the mangy ones.

Maritornes, Mule Driver and Sancho go to the kitchen.

PALOMEQUE

(Appears in the shed) Esteemed señor, my servant girl told me you possess the secret of an all-healing elixir. I'm happy, señor, that fate has brought you to me. I've already given my servant girl all that you've asked for. I hope you will let me try some of this medicine. I've been suffering from lower back pain lately. Just tell me what I need to do to help.

QUIXOTE

It will be my pleasure to fulfill your request, señor castellan.

PALOMEQUE

It's as if my back's being cut with knives.

WORKMAN

(With a mug) Sir?

PALOMEQUE

What do you want?

WORKMAN

To ask for some elixir . . . A huge sty in my eye . . .

PALOMEQUE

That's not going to kill you!

QUIXOTE

Don't chase him away, señor, he's to be pitied. I'll be glad to give him the elixir.

PALOMEQUE

Well, if you're that magnanimous, señor . . .

Enter Maritornes carrying a pot, Sancho, Mule Driver and Don Pedro Martinez's Servant, all with little mugs.

MARITORNES

It's ready, sir.

PALOMEQUE

(To Martinez's Servant) What do you want?

SERVANT

My master, Don Pedro Martinez, heard about the elixir and asks to let him have a dose.

PALOMEQUE

Heh, heh, heh! *(To Servant)* Give me two reals.

SERVANT

Here. The stronger the better. *(Hands Palomeque the money)*

MARITORNES

I made it good and hot, señor!

Don Quixote stretches his hands out over the pot and whispers incantations. Palomeque, Servant and Mule Driver take their hats off.

QUIXOTE

You may drink.

PALOMEQUE

Wait, wait, one at a time!

They fill their mugs with elixir. Martinez's Servant runs off to the wing. The others drink the elixir. Don Quixote is the first to feel sick. He falls on his back.

QUIXOTE

Oh! . . . oh! . . . oh! . . . What is it?!

MARITORNES

Landlord, send for a priest . . . I need to see a priest . . . for all my hard work . . . I'm dying . . .

The music in the wing suddenly stops. There is a clatter of dishes. Laughter is heard.

SANCHO

Cursed be your elixir, now . . . and unto ages of ages, amen! . . .

Palomeque tears from his place and runs off, followed by Maritornes and Workman. Don Pedro Martinez runs out of the wing, followed by his Servant with the mug.

MARTINEZ

Monster! What have you given me to drink?! Hangman!

SERVANT

Two reals, señor, two reals I gave him, like a whole halfpenny . . . The best elixir . . . You told me so yourself!

MARTINEZ

Murderer! *(Runs off)*

SERVANT

What's he so upset about? I better try it.

Finishes the rest of the elixir, stamps his feet in place for a while, then runs off in the wake of Martinez.

SANCHO

What are you doing to people, señor?

Mule Driver slowly drinks the elixir, wipes his mouth, and turns to Sancho.

MULE DRIVER

So it's that bad, is it, my friend?

SANCHO

Leave me alone . . .

MULE DRIVER

I'll tell you what the problem is: not enough pepper, otherwise—a proper elixir. Potent stuff, true, we treat mules with it. Well, first the mule thrashes and kicks a lot, but then he's fit as a fiddle for a whole year and swift as a bolt from a crossbow. Don't worry. You'll feel even worse in a minute, but then you'll jump up and be just fine.

SANCHO

Back off, damn it! You're making me sicker—get the hell away!

MULE DRIVER

It'll pass, friend! Oh-oh! It seems to be working on me, too. *(Exits)*

QUIXOTE

I know why you feel so bad, Sancho: you're not a knight, and this elixir . . .

SANCHO

Why didn't you warn me, señor! . . .

QUIXOTE

And I'm feeling better. All I need is a nap . . .

He falls asleep. Palomeque, Maritornes and Workman come back.

PALOMEQUE

What brought these devils to my inn! I've never seen anything like it in my life!

Martinez enters accompanied by his Servant.

MARTINEZ

You know, it's not bad! First it's a bit scary, but it gets a lot better. Buy another mug from this horse doctor.

SERVANT

Yes, señor.

He goes into the wing with Martinez. Mule Driver comes back to the shed.

SANCHO

Ohh . . . why such punishment? First, two thrashings, then tonight this elixir . . . What is it, señor, do you want to finish me off? What kind of life is this, I ask you?

MULE DRIVER

What thrashings? You said he fell off a cliff.

SANCHO

Leave me alone . . .

It is quickly getting dark, the moon outlines itself. A light appears in Palomeque's window, then goes out. For a while there is laughter, singing, and the clink of glasses in the wing.

MARTINEZ

(In the wing) Drink up, señores!

Then the wing quiets down, the windows turn dark. Maritornes appears in the yard.

MARITORNES

(Sneaking up to the shed) Looks like everybody's asleep. *(Listens)* Yes, asleep ... I'm scared! ... Hey, mule driver, are you sleeping?

QUIXOTE

(Waking up) What's this I hear?

Maritornes in the shed is feeling for Mule Driver's bed. Don Quixote takes her hand.

Lovely señora!

MARITORNES

Is that you? I've come like you asked me to ...

QUIXOTE

Oh, passionate señora, how beholden I would be for the honor you ...

MULE DRIVER

(Waking up) What's going on?

MARITORNES

Ah, the wrong one, the wrong one! It's not you!

QUIXOTE

Fate has flung me, covered with wounds ...

MARITORNES

Let go of me, señor!

QUIXOTE

Señora . . .

MULE DRIVER

Aha! That old goat's a fast one! And he looks like such a pussycat!
Cooks up elixirs, falls off cliffs . . .

QUIXOTE

I understand your intentions . . .

MARITORNES

Let go of me, señor! . . .

QUIXOTE

You must know that I am faithful to the peerless Dulcinea del
Toboso . . .

MULE DRIVER

Oh, to hell with this song and dance!

*Sneaks up to Don Quixote and hits him on the head with a wash
basin.*

QUIXOTE

Oh, perfidious Moor!

MARITORNES

Ah!

SANCHO

(Wakes up) Who's that? Who's that? What are you doing here, my
dear girl? *(Grabs Maritornes by the hand)*

MULE DRIVER

Don't butt into what's none of your business! *(Hits Sancho)*

SANCHO

Here we go again! *(Ducks under the horse blanket)*

QUIXOTE

(Takes his sword) Just you wait, treacherous villain, falling on me from behind! Hey, Sancho!

SANCHO

I'm asleep, sir!

MARITORNES

Where can I go?!

MULE DRIVER

No, not there! The landlord's awake, he'll see you!

There is light in Palomeque's window.

Climb through the roof!

He helps Maritornes to get through the roof, and she disappears from the shed. Mule Driver falls on his bed and covers himself with a horse blanket.

QUIXOTE

The castle's enchanted! There are magicians here! Ah! Here's where you're hiding, wicked creatures! You're many and I'm one, but you won't frighten me! *(Stabs a wineskin with his sword)* See the dark blood pouring out! You're vanquished, villain!

MARTINEZ

(In the wing) What's going on? Light, ho!

HERNANDEZ

(In the wing) Light, light!

Palomeque runs out to the yard.

PALOMEQUE

What's going on in the shed? Hey! I'll bet my life it's that damned Maritornes up to her tricks again! Hey! Maritornes, where are you, you little slut!

QUIXOTE

The enemy is defeated!

MARITORNES

(In the window) What is it? What gets into you at night, landlord?

PALOMEQUE

What? You're here? I was sure you were in the shed!

Hernandez, Martinez with a sword, his Servant with a poker, and another guest with a lantern come running into the yard.

MARTINEZ

Who's there? What's happening? Anybody killed?

HERNANDEZ

Thieves? Where are the thieves? Hey, you in the shed! . . .

Dawn is breaking.

QUIXOTE

My enemy is slain, esteemed castellan! See the blood pouring from him!

PALOMEQUE

(Dropping his lantern) I wish it was your blood instead! Look, señores, this madman stabbed a wineskin!

MULE DRIVER

(Pretending he is just waking up) Ah, why the hell can't you let people sleep!

SANCHO

Right! Why can't you let us sleep, me and my knight?

QUIXOTE

The others have fled, Sancho! Quick, let's go, we'll catch them!

SANCHO

Yes, señor, it's a good time to go. There's big trouble coming.

He runs to the stable, brings out Rocinante and the donkey. Workman and Maritornes enter.

PALOMEQUE

Just look what this pair of half-wits have done, señores! My best wine!

HERNANDEZ

They're really some kind of devils! Isn't that so, Señor Martinez?

MARTINEZ

Is it the one who made the elixir?

SERVANT

The very same, sir.

MARTINEZ

An excellent elixir. Only what the hell got into them during the night?

QUIXOTE

(Mounted) Señor castellan, I'm desolate that I must hasten to leave your hospitable castle. I have to set out in pursuit of my enemies.

Thank you for your attentiveness to me and my squire. With all my best wishes.

MULE DRIVER

There he goes again! He ought to get it in the neck and good riddance!

SANCHO

There's no need for long speeches, señor. Let's go.

PALOMEQUE

You can keep your gratitude, mister apothecary. Just pay for your room, your board, and above all for the wine you wasted at my inn!

QUIXOTE

You mean this is an inn? Is it true? So I was deluded in supposing I was in a castle. But, anyhow, it doesn't matter. Scorching heat, freezing cold, the foulest weather torment knights errant as they wander through the world for the good of mankind, and never anywhere has anyone dared to demand any sort of payment from them. Such is the rule of the order. Good-bye.

PALOMEQUE

Stop! Justice, señores!

QUIXOTE

(Threatening him with his lance) Out of my way, if you cherish your life, greedy innkeeper!

Rides through the gate.

PALOMEQUE

Justice! Justice! I've been robbed! Hold the other one! *(To Workman)* Shut the gate!

Sancho is surrounded.

Will you pay or not, you crook?

SANCHO

Scorching heat . . . torments our order . . . Let me pass!

PALOMEQUE

See what thieves they are, señores?

HERNANDEZ

Shall we teach the bastard a lesson?

MARTINEZ

I repeat: the elixir's excellent, but the man's a real swindler! Where's the blanket!

SANCHO

Help, señor! . . . Don't run away, you contemptible creatures! Help! . . .

Don Quixote's head appears above the fence. They all fall upon Sancho and throw him down on the blanket.

QUIXOTE

(Behind the fence) Vile scoundrels! Let my squire go at once!

Sancho is tossed in the blanket.

PALOMEQUE

(During a pause) Are you going to pay up?

SANCHO

I'd be very happy to, but I can't . . .

PALOMEQUE

Toss him sky high!

MARTINEZ

Enough! To hell with him!

PALOMEQUE

(Seizing Sancho's wineskin) Give me your wineskin and get out of my sight, you dirty crook!

They all leave the courtyard, except for Maritornes and Mule Driver.

MULE DRIVER

I like that guy! He's stubborn. He didn't pay. Good for him!

MARITORNES

(To Sancho) Here, drink some water.

QUIXOTE

(Outside the fence) Don't drink that water, Sancho, it's been poisoned. I still have a glassful of elixir. It'll set you on your feet in no time.

SANCHO

Keep your elixir for Reinaldo de Montalbán, señor, for the golden idol of Mohammed, and for who the hell else! And leave me alone!

QUIXOTE

Poor man! I can't watch you poisoning yourself! Come to your senses.

He rides away from the fence.

SANCHO

Bring me some wine, miss. *(Whispers)* You I'll pay.

Maritornes brings wine.

MULE DRIVER

Give me some to keep him company.

SANCHO

Thank you.

He gives Maritornes a coin.

MULE DRIVER

No, don't, it's my treat. I like you—you've got guts.

SANCHO

You're the only kind people in this inn full of tormentors. It's obvious, miss, that your behavior is a bit questionable. But I don't like to judge people. Thank you, and good-bye.

MARITORNES

Good-bye.

Mule Driver accompanies Sancho to the gate.

MULE DRIVER

You should put in more pepper. Don't forget that. Then you'd have no problem charging one real per mug.

Scene 2

At Don Quixote's. Daytime. Antonia, Housekeeper, Pérez and Nicholas are in the room.

PÉREZ

So what do we do now? It's not for nothing they say—fight fire with fire.

NICHOLAS

My dear friend, I agree with you completely.

PÉREZ

A yearning to do great things drove the poor hidalgo from home. Let's give him the chance to do some great deed that will bring him back again. Here is what Señor Nicholas and I have come up with: you, Antonia, will assume the role of an enchanted princess.

ANTONIA

I don't understand, señor.

NICHOLAS

It's all in here, let's open this up—and you'll understand everything.

He takes from a bundle a sumptuous woman's dress, a big tie-on beard, a guitar and some masks.

PÉREZ

Remember, Antonia, that you are an enchanted princess, the daughter of King Tinacrio the Wise and Queen Jaramilla, heiress to the great kingdom of Micomicon in Guinea. The wicked giant Cross-eyed Pandafilando took your kingdom from you. Now we will go in pursuit of your mad uncle, and then with tears in your eyes, you will beg him to protect you and to win back your kingdom from the giant.

HOUSEKEEPER

God have mercy on us!

NICHOLAS

And if he doesn't follow you wherever you like, I'm not the village barber!

PÉREZ

But you must make it clear to him that the way to your kingdom runs through La Mancha.

ANTONIA

Ah, now I understand!

Nicholas gives Antonia the dress and a mask.

NICHOLAS

Disguise yourself, Antonia.

ANTONIA

One moment. *(Exits to the neighboring room)*

HOUSEKEEPER

Merciful heavens, what tricks we have to play to bring our poor master back to his own hearth! May the devil and robber Barabbas take down into netherworld those books of chivalry that have ruined the brightest mind in La Mancha! And, along with the books, that fat-bellied Sancho, who lured Señor Alonso away from home! *(Exits)*

PÉREZ

Let's get on with it, my dear friend.

Pérez ties on the beard. Nicholas puts on a woman's dress, headgear and a mask, and takes the guitar. Antonia enters in the sumptuous dress, wearing a mask.

ANTONIA

Is that you, Master Nicholas? What are you now?

NICHOLAS

I'm a duenna accompanying you in your sorrowful exile. Remember my name—Dolorida. *(Strums the guitar)*

PÉREZ

And I am your uncle, Señora Antonia, the brother of the slain King Tinacrio.

ANTONIA

I see, I see!

PÉREZ

The only important thing is to lure him here. Then we'll think up something, depending on the circumstances.

Just then Sancho comes riding into the yard on his donkey. At the same moment, Housekeeper runs out from the kitchen.

HOUSEKEEPER

It's him! Yes, it's him! If my old eyes aren't deceiving me!

SANCHO

Yes, it's me, señora housekeeper.

HOUSEKEEPER

It's him, the troublemaker, the globe-trotting tramp!

SANCHO

Yes, it's her . . .

Antonia, Pérez and Nicholas rush to the window to watch the scene.

HOUSEKEEPER

Answer me, you paltry parrot repeating other people's words: where is Señor Quixano? Where have you put him? Are you alone? Answer me: have you come back alone?

SANCHO

I'm not so stupid, señora housekeeper, as to claim there are two of us. You can see I'm alone.

HOUSEKEEPER

What have you done to Señor Alonso, you sinner?

SANCHO

Some good-hearted person, help me! My dear housekeeper, I have
been beaten many times these past few days, but each time it was
towards the end of our stay in some place. Now the drubbing has
begun the moment I poke my nose through the gate! Help!

ANTONIA

Oh, God! She's tearing him to pieces!

PÉREZ

Wait, wait, we'll find out everything now.

HOUSEKEEPER

What have you done to my master?

SANCHO

Save me from this fiend of a housekeeper! The señor is alive and
well! You have no right to beat me! I'm going to be a governor one
of these days!

HOUSEKEEPER

Have you ever heard the like, good people? Who told you that, you
greedy blockhead? Where is Señor Quixano? Why are you silent?

SANCHO

God in Heaven! Won't anybody save me from the hands of this
housekeeper, who's tearing at me like a hawk at a chicken?!

PÉREZ

Señora housekeeper! . . . Dear señora, hold back your wrath. This
man is innocent!

SANCHO

Who's this?

HOUSEKEEPER

Just let him tell me where he left Señor Alonso!

PÉREZ

We'll find that out sooner than you will. I strongly advise you, señora housekeeper, to go back to preparing our food, we have a long journey ahead of us.

HOUSEKEEPER

Very well, señor. But I beg you, find out where my poor master is! *(Exits)*

PÉREZ

Honored sir, please leave your donkey and come in here.

SANCHO

(Entering the room) Good health to you, worthy señoras and señor!

PÉREZ

Why, it's—him!

NICHOLAS

I can't believe my eyes.

PÉREZ

Yes, princess, it's him, Sancho Panza, squire to the famous knight Don Quixote. I won't rest till I've embraced him!

ANTONIA

No, no, let me be the first!

NICHOLAS

No, me first. *(Embraces Sancho)* My woman's soul is stirred. The only thing that might calm me is music.

He plays the guitar. Pérez and Antonia embrace Sancho.

SANCHO

I humbly thank you for the music and for the kindness you've showered upon me. But tell me, how do you know who I am?

PÉREZ

The fame of your knight is spreading through the world like fire through a forest—followed, of course, by your own fame as well. Sit down, our most beloved of all squires, and tell us: where is your knight now?

SANCHO

I'm very happy to sit down, because I'm very tired after the house-keeper's beating, but I won't tell you where my master is.

PÉREZ

Why not?

ANTONIA

What's this I hear? The cruel squire wants to rob me of my last hope?

NICHOLAS

Why don't you want to reveal to us where your master is?

SANCHO

Because he told me to keep it a secret.

NICHOLAS

It's strange, my dear squire! The two of you left together, and you come back alone. For all I know, people may think you killed Señor Quixote.

SANCHO

Let each of us be killed by his own fate, dear lady, but I'd never have done that and everybody knows it.

ANTONIA

No, he'll tell us where Don Quixote is. You should know, Sancho, that this is Princess Micomicon standing before you!

DON QUIXOTE

SANCHO

Ahh! That's very interesting. Never in my whole life have I seen a princess.

ANTONIA

Now I hope you will confide to me the whereabouts of your knight, whom I am seeking in order to ask for his help and protection.

SANCHO

No, princess, I will not confide it to you.

ANTONIA

Listen, then, you wicked squire, to the sad story of my life. I lived in indescribable luxury in the royal palace of my unforgettable father Tinacrio the Wise and his now inconsolable brother . . .

PÉREZ

That's me, here before you.

ANTONIA

Yes, it's him. I received royal honors. I sat on a golden throne by day, and at night princes sang serenades in the park under my windows.

Nicholas plays the guitar.

SANCHO

Your story is very interesting, princess, but I see nothing sad in it.

ANTONIA

Listen further, poor man! One terrible day the host of the giant Pandafilando attacked our kingdom . . .

SANCHO

Ah! That's not so good! . . . I can picture that . . . A small gang of Yangües herdsmen attacked us once . . . and to this day I . . . however, it's not worth talking about. So what happened next?

167

ANTONIA

My mother, Queen Jaramilla . . . and my father . . .

SANCHO

That same Tinacrio?

ANTONIA

Yes, yes. Cut down!

SANCHO

Both killed?

ANTONIA

Yes, they're both in their grave.

SANCHO

(To Pérez) And you, the king's brother, how did you manage to survive? You probably surrendered? In desperate situations, the bravest one saves himself for a better occasion.

NICHOLAS

(To Pérez) What a pain in the neck!

PÉREZ

(To Nicholas) I think he's a bit moved.

Nicholas plays the guitar.

ANTONIA

And so, accompanied by my duenna, I went rushing in search of Don Quixote de la Mancha, to seek protection with him. Now you'll surely tell me where he is?

SANCHO

No, I won't.

NICHOLAS

(Flinging the guitar aside) Oh, damn it all!

PÉREZ

My dearest duenna Dolorida, you're wrong to be angry. I think the squire is right to keep the secret entrusted to him by his master. But tell me, my good Sancho Panza, what brings you here alone?

SANCHO

I'm bringing a letter from my master to his niece.

PÉREZ

She left along with the priest and the barber . . .

SANCHO

I know him, his name is Nicholas.

NICHOLAS

Right, with Nicholas. An excellent man, that Nicholas!

SANCHO

He's really tricky.

NICHOLAS

Now, now, now . . .

PÉREZ

Wait . . . they left for town, in search of her lost uncle. Is it an important letter?

SANCHO

A very important one and, above all, a pleasant one.

PÉREZ

You don't say! . . .

SANCHO

It contains an order to give me two donkey colts in reward for my faithful service. *(Feels in his pockets)* Ah!... Ah!... Ah!!

PÉREZ

What's wrong?

SANCHO

Oh, I'm such a miserable idiot, a Don Moron! A brute, a swine! Curse me! *(Slaps himself in the face)* Take that! Take that!

ANTONIA

What's wrong, squire?

NICHOLAS

What's wrong, my dear, stubborn fellow?

SANCHO

Beat me, señores, I beg you, hit me, it's hard hitting yourself! I lost the letter, which means I've lost the colts too. I rode all night, dreaming of how happy my Juana Teresa would be to have them! Oh, my darling donkeys! I was trembling with joy, I already seemed to feel you in my hands, I caressed your soft fur, I could see you in my barn. Without that letter, who will believe that my master really gave me those donkeys? Pandafilando, why didn't you slay me instead of Tinacrio the Wise?

PÉREZ

Yes, that's bad.

NICHOLAS

Yes, you'll have to part with your dream about the donkeys! *(Plays the guitar)*

SANCHO

Stop playing! What an awful habit! As soon as something nasty happens, you pick up your guitar!

PÉREZ

Calm down, Sancho. I know who can help you in your despair. It is she, the good-hearted Princess Micomicon. She need only say a word to the housekeeper—and you'll have your donkeys.

SANCHO

The fiendish housekeeper will listen to her?

PÉREZ

I promise you that. But it goes without saying that, after this great favor, you'll tell us where Don Quixote is hiding.

SANCHO

(Reflecting) All right.

ANTONIA

Oh, kind squire! *(Through the window)* Señora housekeeper! Señora housekeeper!

Pérez, Nicholas and Sancho all look through the window.

HOUSEKEEPER

What do you want?

ANTONIA

My dear housekeeper: be so good as to hand two donkey colts over to Sancho, on Señor Alonso's orders.

HOUSEKEEPER

What? What? What did you say? Two donkeys?

SANCHO

Unh-hunh!

HOUSEKEEPER

I'd sooner give up my soul than give this scoundrel . . .

SANCHO

Unh-hunh! What did I tell you!

PÉREZ

(Softly, through the window) If you wish to see Señor Alonso, you'd better immediately . . .

HOUSEKEEPER

This . . . this . . . what's his name? . . . Sancho? Well, I'll gladly give him two donkeys. Come here, you vil . . . come here, Sancho, open the barn, take the donkeys. My God, what have we come to? *(Disappears)*

SANCHO

Oh, joy! Oh, joy, and joy again! To tell the truth, I didn't believe you, but now I'm convinced that you are indeed Princess Micomicon!

PÉREZ

Yes, but don't forget to tell us where Don Quixote is hiding.

SANCHO

In a canyon in the Sierra Morena.

ANTONIA

What's he doing there?

SANCHO

He decided to go and be a madman in the mountains, because of the cruelty of Dulcinea del Toboso, in imitation of Rotolando and Amadís. I'll show you the way.

ANTONIA

Let's set out at once, before something bad happens to him.

SANCHO

Allow me to embrace you, dear brother of Tinacrio the Wise!

He embraces Pérez, whose beard comes off.

Ah, what's this?! Señor padre?

NICHOLAS

(Embracing Sancho) What? Who? What padre? Where? *(Reattaches the beard)*

SANCHO

Joy clouded my eyes, and I fancied that Pandafilando tore off your beard and instead of you there was the padre! But I see now that I imagined it! . . . Oh, joy!

He runs out to the yard, runs to the barn, opens the door.

Here they are, here they are, my precious ones! *(Shouts)* For some reason, lady, you've stopped playing the guitar!

Nicholas plays the guitar. The sound of a rolling wagon is heard.

ANTONIA

To the Sierra Morena!

PÉREZ

To the Sierra Morena!

Curtain.

ACT THREE

___

Scene 1

At Don Quixote's. Daytime. An enormous carriage drives up to the gate, carrying Don Quixote, the disguised Antonia, Pérez and Nicholas. Nicholas sits on the box beside the driver and plays the guitar. Sancho follows on his donkey. The last to appear is Rocinante, tied to Sancho's saddle. Housekeeper comes running from the kitchen.

HOUSEKEEPER
Señor Alonso! At last! At last! How happy all our loving hearts are that you have finally agreed to come home! Ah, Señor Alonso! At last!

QUIXOTE
My good housekeeper!

Antonia, Pérez and Nicholas help the limping Don Quixote down from the carriage. The carriage drives off. Sancho makes for the stable with his donkey and Rocinante.

175

Most Serene Princess, allow me to introduce our esteemed house-keeper.

ANTONIA

Very pleased to meet you.

QUIXOTE

(Making introductions) Duenna . . . my housekeeper . . . I'm sure you will love each other at first sight.

NICHOLAS

I have dreamt of this meeting! *(Embraces Housekeeper)*

QUIXOTE

Kindly come in, my dear guests.

Antonia, Pérez and Nicholas bow and go in.

Where is Antonia?

HOUSEKEEPER

Antonia is inside, sir, and already receiving that princess what's-her-name and the bearded fellow.

QUIXOTE

(Sitting on a bench) Shh! . . . he's not some bearded fellow, he's the princess's high-ranking, though very unfortunate, uncle. I'm still struck by the tragedy of his brother, the king of Guinea, who was killed by Cross-eyed Pandafilando.

HOUSEKEEPER

God be with him, my dear señor! So the Guinean got killed, what can we do! Serves him right! You can't resurrect him, can you? And I killed two of my best fat chickens to make bouillon for you, and that will really be of more use to you than the king of Guinea!

ANTONIA

(Dressed as usual, runs out of the house) My priceless uncle! I'm so happy you've come back!

QUIXOTE

Antonia! Have you taken proper care of the princess and her duenna?

ANTONIA

Of course, Uncle! Don't you hear the duenna already playing the guitar in my room?

SANCHO

(Coming from the shed) So she is, and may God not deprive her of eternal salvation! But I'd be glad if some enchanted Moor stole her guitar! She plays it all the time on the slightest pretext.

QUIXOTE

You have a somewhat crude character, Sancho. One should love music. Where there's music, there's no evil.

SANCHO

You can even get sick of roast pigeon, master, if you eat them from morning till night. That music makes me want to run screaming out of the house. Allow me to leave you for a short time, señor, I'd like to visit my Teresa.

HOUSEKEEPER

Go, go, Sancho, nobody's keeping you.

QUIXOTE

Go, my friend, but come back soon.

HOUSEKEEPER

(In a whisper) Go and don't come back. Understand?

SANCHO

But master . . .

HOUSEKEEPER

Don't come back, if you want to keep what's left of that beard. You know me.

SANCHO

Who doesn't? . . . A nice vise I'm caught in! *(Exits)*

QUIXOTE

Well, Antonia, let's go in.

He goes into the house accompanied by Antonia. Housekeeper goes to the kitchen. Inside, Antonia helps Don Quixote out of his armor, sits him down. Pérez enters from the inner rooms in his ordinary guise.

PÉREZ

Greetings, my dear friend. Nicholas and I learned of your return and have come at once to pay our respects.

QUIXOTE

I'm so glad to see you, my dear padre. Antonia, invite the king's brother here. I want him to meet Señor Pero Pérez.

ANTONIA

At once, Uncle!

She goes and begins to kiss Don Quixote. Meanwhile, Pérez escapes to the inner rooms.

I'll call him at once, Uncle.

She goes to the inner rooms.
    Pérez peeks through the door in his beard.

PÉREZ

Señor Don Quixote . . .

QUIXOTE

Ah, Your Highness! I beg you to come in!

PÉREZ

(In the doorway) I'm not properly dressed, Señor Don Quixote . . .

QUIXOTE

Never mind, never mind, you're traveling, nobody will say anything.

Pérez disappears.

Señor padre, allow me to introduce the king's brother. Excuse me, where's the padre? He was just here!

He goes to the front door. Pérez, without a beard, enters from the inner rooms.

PÉREZ

Here I am, Señor Don Quixote.

QUIXOTE

What wonders! I lost you! Did you go somewhere?

PÉREZ

Wouldn't think of it!

QUIXOTE

Ehh . . . I'm more and more convinced that there's something suspicious going on here! Antonia, where have you gone?

ANTONIA

(Enters in the princess's costume and mask) I beg your pardon, valiant knight, for being late . . .

179

QUIXOTE

Allow me, charming Princess Micomicon, to introduce my friend,
Señor Pero Pérez.

PÉREZ

Delighted, princess.

ANTONIA

I've heard so much about you!

NICHOLAS

(Enters in the costume of the duenna) And here I am, valiant knight!

QUIXOTE

Ah, we're all together at last! No, the king's esteemed but whimsi-
cal brother isn't here.

PÉREZ

I'll bring him at once. *(Exits to inner rooms)*

QUIXOTE

And where is Master Nicholas?

PÉREZ

(Enters in the guise of the king's brother) Here I am at last.

Nicholas escapes to the inner rooms.

QUIXOTE

Mister king's brother, I would like to introduce you to my friends—
the priest and the barber. Master Nicholas!

Nicholas comes out in his usual guise. Antonia disappears.

PÉREZ

So this is the virtuous barber you've told me so much about! Just
as I imagined him!

NICHOLAS

And I, in turn, wept bitterly, listening to the horrors Pandafilando wreaked upon your brother's kingdom!

QUIXOTE

Antonia, do come here!

Antonia enters in her usual guise.

ANTONIA

Here I am, Uncle!

Pérez disappears behind Don Quixote's armchair.

QUIXOTE

I want to hear about the woes that befell the king's family from the lips of the king's brother. Señor padre, please come closer.

Pérez peeks from behind the armchair without the beard.

PÉREZ

I'm listening with the greatest attention.

He hides behind the armchair, then peeks out with the beard on.

Yes, it's as if that loathsome giant were still standing before my eyes!

He hides behind the armchair, takes the beard off, places himself in front of Don Quixote.

Such things you tell of, esteemed king's brother!

NICHOLAS

(To Antonia) We're in big trouble!

ANTONIA

(To Nicholas) Quick, bring on the magician! *(To Don Quixote)* Yes, yes ... such terrible things, Uncle!

Pérez comes from behind the armchair in the beard.

PÉREZ

I'd better cut my story short, my gentle señora niece, since it troubles you so much.

ANTONIA

Ah, no, no, go on!

QUIXOTE

Yes, go on, only I'd like you all to sit down, because I must confess things are spinning in my eyes for some reason ...

Nicholas escapes to the next room. Pérez rushes to the window.

... and sometimes I don't even know who's standing in front of me.

A clatter of broken dishes offstage. Pérez closes the shutters, the room becomes dark.

What's that? What's happening?

NICHOLAS

(Offstage) Help! The magician's here!

PÉREZ

Help!

QUIXOTE

(Seizing his sword) Where is he?

NICHOLAS

(Running in) The magician abducted Princess Micomicon right
in front of my eyes!

PÉREZ

Where is the king's brother?

ANTONIA

The duenna's not here either!

QUIXOTE

This was to be expected! We were carried away with our conversation, and the perfidious one suddenly came flying! My squire!
Pursue them!

PÉREZ

Useless, useless, Señor Don Quixote! As if you could fly through
the air after them!

NICHOLAS

I saw him myself, in a black cloak, flying over the house, dragging
the king's brother by the beard!

QUIXOTE

Why didn't you cut his arm off?

NICHOLAS

I missed!

QUIXOTE

Ah, I'll never forgive myself! Where were the guards? Bring me my
shield and my horse!

ANTONIA

Uncle, dear, I beg you—calm yourself.

QUIXOTE

I vowed to protect the princess! Let me pass! You're stricken with
fear, but I'm not afraid, and I'll catch up with him even if he flies
like the wind! Don't hold me back!

He drops his sword, sinks into armchair.

ANTONIA

What's the matter, Uncle?

QUIXOTE

My wounds have opened . . . I suddenly feel weak . . . he's put a
spell on me . . .

ANTONIA

Uncle, listen to the voice of a loving niece. You must rest and
recover your strength. My precious uncle, listen to me!

PÉREZ

Listen to us, señor knight. Go to bed. Beneficent sleep will fortify
you.

QUIXOTE

Yes . . . Right now I'm unable to move from the spot . . . Sorcery has
fettered me with its chains . . .

*Antonia and Pérez lead Don Quixote to his bed and lie him down
on it.*

ANTONIA

(Closing the bed curtains) He's asleep. Poor, poor Uncle!

PÉREZ

You mustn't despair, señora. Sleep will refresh him and perhaps
he'll be calmer when he wakes up. Let's go, Master Nicholas.
Good-bye, señora niece. We'll come to call on him in the evening.

ANTONIA

Good-bye, señores. I thank you from the bottom of my heart for all you've done for my uncle.

PÉREZ

We only did our duty.

He exits with Nicholas. Antonia goes down to the kitchen. Shortly afterward, Sansón Carrasco comes through the gate from the road.

SANSÓN

Here it is. The courtyard so dear to my heart! For two years I've been away from my birthplace, and yet nothing has changed . . . The bench where Antonia and I sat two years ago . . . Anybody home? . . . Hello!

Enter Housekeeper and Antonia.

ANTONIA

Ah!

HOUSEKEEPER

Can it be . . . ?

SANSÓN

It's me, it's me, my dearest señora housekeeper!

HOUSEKEEPER

Good God, look at you. The son of the simple peasant Bartolomeo Carrasco—now a learned man and an important gentleman! Ah, Sansón, I can't reach so high as you now!

ANTONIA

You probably won't want to know us now, Sansón—that is, *Señor* Carrasco?

185

SANSÓN

Dear housekeeper, you're right about only one thing: I really have become a scholar. Before you stands a graduate of the University of Salamanca—in my breast pocket I have four learned degrees, with highest honors! But no, housekeeper, I have not become so important! And to prove it, allow me to hug you!

HOUSEKEEPER

Ah, Sansón, it makes me so happy to see that you're not puffed up with pride, and you're as nice to your old friends as you were before!

SANSÓN

Antonia! How pretty you've grown! No, no, pride is foreign to me, even if I had twenty degrees! *(Tries to hug Antonia)*

ANTONIA

Señor scholar!

HOUSEKEEPER

Ah, there's no harm in that; he's not a stranger, he's from our village. You were nourished by the same earth, warmed by the same sun!

SANSÓN

I'm just excited to be in my native village again, and especially to see you again, Antonia.

He rushes to embrace Antonia, but she dodges him and he embraces Housekeeper.

And you, too, dear housekeeper!

He reaches his hand out to Antonia, kisses her hand.

I saw you more than once in my dreams.

HOUSEKEEPER
And I you, dear Sansón!

SANSÓN
And you, Antonia, aren't you at least a little happy to see me?

ANTONIA
Yes, I'm happy . . . very happy . . .

HOUSEKEEPER
And I am, too.

They both suddenly burst into tears.

SANSÓN
And this is how you show it? What's the matter?

ANTONIA
My uncle has gone mad.

SANSÓN
What are you saying?!

HOUSEKEEPER
Those cursed books darkened the mind of the kindest and most intelligent of men!

ANTONIA
He put on rusty armor and ran away from home to fight some giants and save princesses . . . Stuck a barber's bowl on his head, waved a sword . . . He got our neighbor Sancho Panza completely addled, calling him his squire, and he ran away with him! We barely managed to bring him back by playing a trick . . . Sansón is probably hungry, señora housekeeper. Why don't you give our guest something to eat?

HOUSEKEEPER

Of course he should eat now that he's back with us! Dinner will be ready soon. *(Goes to kitchen)*

SANSÓN

Your grief touches me deeply, dear Antonia!

ANTONIA

You've always been smart, and now you're also a scholar. If you can think up a way of getting us out of this trouble, I'll give you a kiss, Sansón!

SANSÓN

What's that? A kiss? You know, I already have a plan! Kiss me, Antonia!

ANTONIA

Are you telling the truth?

SANSÓN

I've never been known to lie, have I, Antonia?

ANTONIA

I think you're telling the truth, Sansón!

Antonia kisses Sansón, and at the same moment Sancho's head appears above the fence.

SANSÓN

Damn it all, there's that Sancho!

ANTONIA

The man himself.

SANSÓN

My plan is ripening. Leave me alone with him, Antonia.

DON QUIXOTE

ANTONIA

All right, all right, I trust you, Sansón! *(Goes to kitchen door, turns)*
Sansón . . .

SANSÓN

Another kiss, Antonia!

Sancho's head appears above the fence again.

ANTONIA

Later. *(Disappears)*

SANSÓN

Why so shy, my dear sir? Come in, since you're here.

SANCHO

Is that viper around?

SANSÓN

Who do you mean?

SANCHO

Who else could I mean? The housekeeper, of course.

SANSÓN

She's in the kitchen.

Sancho leads his donkey in and puts him in the corner.

So it's you, my dear Sancho Panza?

SANCHO

Unless this is a trick of the foul magician Friston, it's my compatriot Sansón, son of old Bartolomeo, I see before me?

189

SANSÓN

God save us from magicians! Yes, it's me!

SANCHO

I'll be damned, so you're a scholar now, Sansón! *(Kisses him)*

SANSÓN

But tell me, dear neighbor, what's happened to half your beard?

SANCHO

Don't speak of rope in the hanged man's house, Señor Carrasco. Didn't you learn that in your university? God grant there are as many coins jingling in your pocket as I had clumps of my beard pulled out in the past week!

SANSÓN

That's very sad, Señor Panza, but I hope you'll grow a new one and it will be even more flourishing than before.

SANCHO

And I in turn hope that your learning will flourish as much as my future beard.

SANSÓN

Eh, what a witty reply! Did you go to Salamanca, by any chance?

SANCHO

I don't need any Salamanca. I even hope to become a governor very soon without any of that.

SANSÓN

How? Teach me! I want to become a governor, too.

SANCHO

There's nothing I can do to teach you. It won't help. For that you have to become the squire to the great knight Don Quixote de la Mancha!

SANSÓN

Yes, madness is contagious, I can see it now.

SANCHO

What did you say?

SANSÓN

It was an aside.

SANCHO

Then keep it aside.

QUIXOTE

(Wakes up) Sancho! Come here!

SANCHO

Hear that? My master's calling me.

SANSÓN

Very good. Take me to him, Sancho.

He goes into the house with Sancho.

SANCHO

Señor, there's a visitor to see you.

QUIXOTE

Very glad.

SANSÓN

Señor Don Quixote de la Mancha, allow me to give you my greetings! Your fame has spread and reached the ears of your humble servant and modest compatriot, the scholar Sansón Carrasco.

QUIXOTE

Are you the son of Bartolomeo Carrasco?

SANSÓN

Exactly so, señor.

QUIXOTE

I am very happy to see before me a compatriot who has reached such a high level of learning.

SANSÓN

Still happier am I to be the guest of a knight, the fame of whose exploits resounds throughout the land.

QUIXOTE

Sit down, señor scholar. You are visiting me at a moment of terrible misfortune . . .

SANSÓN

It grieves me to hear it, señor.

QUIXOTE

My eternal enemy, the perfidious magician Friston—there's no need to tell a learned man like yourself who he is, you must have read about him a hundred times—he has just abducted an unfortunate orphan from my house, Princess Micomicon, who has been under my protection, as well as her charming royal uncle and the duenna Dolorida!

SANCHO

(In despair) Abindaraez de Vargas! . . . A curse on me and all my relations! *(Throws down his hat)*

QUIXOTE

You see, señor scholar, the news has plunged even this—I must admit—crude nature into despair.

SANCHO

How should I not be plunged into despair, if a governorship has just slipped from my fingers? I already had hold of a governor's coattail, dreaming of how you'd crush the giant's army, and the kingdom would be ours!

QUIXOTE
That, señor scholar, is what has happened.

SANSÓN
I'm astounded! What do you intend to do?

QUIXOTE
I will immediately set out in pursuit of them.

SANSÓN
And your decision is irrevocable?

QUIXOTE
How can you ask that, scholar? It is my debt of honor!

SANCHO
Well, naturally, you're not some sort of Yangüeso!

SANSÓN
What?

SANCHO
Never mind . . . there was this incident, it's not worth talking about it . . . fifteen men against two, pulling out half a beard.

SANSÓN
My God! *(To Don Quixote)* But where are you going to search for this princess and her abductor?

QUIXOTE
Some good magician sent me a dream, which has convinced me that the villain was headed northeast, towards the Duke's domain. I'll go there. Sancho, arm me!

Sancho begins to put armor on Don Quixote.

SANSÓN

Tell me, señor, what if fate smiles unkindly on you and your adversaries defeat you?

QUIXOTE

If I fall in single combat, I will accept my adversary's conditions, just as he will accept mine if I'm victorious.

SANSÓN

Go at once, my lord Don Quixote!

QUIXOTE

Señor scholar, your understanding of matters of honor is the same as mine. Sancho, my horse!

They go out to the courtyard. Antonia and Housekeeper come out of the kitchen, Housekeeper carrying a dish.

HOUSEKEEPER

Oh no! Señor Alonso's put his armor on again! And that fat miscreant is already leading his donkey out—may it break its four legs!

SANCHO

Señora housekeeper ... I humbly beg you ...

He hastily rides through the gate.

QUIXOTE

Farewell, Antonia! Farewell, señora housekeeper!

HOUSEKEEPER

Oh, dear God! Once again, the gates of madness are thrown open before him, and he rushes through them to perish with his eyes shut!

ANTONIA

What are you doing, Señor Alonso! Come to your senses! Sansón, talk him out of it! You promised!

QUIXOTE

(In the saddle) So, señor scholar, are you going to talk me out of doing as honor requires?

SANSÓN

Never in my life! Go, my lord Don Quixote de la Mancha, I warmly wish you luck!

QUIXOTE

Farewell, my faithful children! I know you love me, but don't detain me any longer, and don't grieve over me.

He rides off.

HOUSEKEEPER

I have no words to tell you what I think of you! So this is how you deal with our grief? You pushed that unfortunate madman through the gate with your own hands! Learning must have eaten up what was left of your conscience. You not only can't sympathize with poor people in their misery, but you even made fun of them!

SANSÓN

Don't rush to condemn me, hear me out first.

HOUSEKEEPER

I don't want to hear you out! Curse the University of Salamanca! *(Runs out the gate after Don Quixote)* Señor Alonso! Stop, by all that's holy! ...

SANSÓN

Antonia!

ANTONIA

Don't come near me, Sansón! I can't believe my own eyes and ears! Did you really mean to hurt us like this? Why, tell me? What have we poor people done to you?

SANSÓN

Antonia!

ANTONIA

Coward. Just to please Señor Alonso, you urge him to new recklessness instead of stopping him. You deceived me, Sansón!

SANSÓN

Oh, be quiet! Me a coward? You'll see what sort of coward I am, Antonia, and you'll bitterly regret your words. I told you I'll save him, you foolish girl, and so I will!

ANTONIA

I no longer believe you!

SANSÓN

Don't go mad yourself, Antonia, and don't insult me! I'll follow him and bring him home—for good! If I don't succeed, I'll never come back! That would be a pity, Antonia, because I rushed home in order to see you! Well, so, it means I'll never see you again! I've got no time for talking now, I'm afraid to lose the trail. Farewell, Antonia! *(Runs off)*

ANTONIA

Sansón! Sansón! I believe you! What are you going to do!

SANSÓN

(From far off) I can't tell you . . .

HOUSEKEEPER

(Far off) Señor Alonso, stop! . . .

Scene 2

Daytime. A hall in Duke's palace.
Duke enters.

DUKE

To me! Ho!

Servants come running.

We'll be having guests in the castle: that madman who calls himself Don Quixote de la Mancha and his squire. Receive him with all honors, and let nobody dare show any doubt of his being a knight errant. *(To Majordomo)* I ask you and *(To Doctor Aguero)* you to go to my country seat and prepare everything for receiving his squire as governor. Tell him he is on the island of Barataria. The Duchess and I will arrive in a few days to have a look at all he's done.

MAJORDOMO

Very good, Your Grace.

Doctor Aguero, Majordomo and several pages exit.
Duenna Rodriguez, several other duennas and pages remain.
The sound of horns. Duchess enters, hands her falcon to a page. She is followed by Don Quixote and Sancho.

DUCHESS

Welcome to our house, Lord Don Quixote!

QUIXOTE

(In doorway) After you, Your Grace!

Sancho enters first.

Most gracious Duchess, forgive this ignoramus!

197

DUCHESS

Don't worry, señor, his artlessness and lack of self-consciousness are very sweet.

DUKE

I'm glad, Señor Don Quixote, to be able to receive you as befits a knight.

QUIXOTE

I'm very pleased, Your Grace. *(To Sancho)* If you disgrace me again, you eternal blockhead and buffoon, I'll have your head!

SANCHO

Did I do something wrong, señor? I promise to behave properly from now on, so from now on if there's a slipup, it's not my fault.

QUIXOTE

Silence!

DUKE

Kindly come this way, my lord, to wash up after your journey.

Duchess exits.

Sancho, help your master.

SANCHO

After you, Your Grace. *(Turning to the duenna Rodriguez)* Madame, I left my donkey by the gate. Tell someone to take him to the stable, or, better still, do it yourself. I wouldn't entrust him to just anybody. Watch out though, he's very skittish.

RODRIGUEZ

You're out of your mind.

SANCHO

Me? No. My master told me that the knight Lansarot was attended by lords and his horse—by ladies. True, I came on a donkey, but, by God, he's worth any horse.

RODRIGUEZ

What a joke! An ass comes to our castle riding an ass! So I, the duenna Rodriguez, should take a donkey to the stable? How's this! *(Insults him by biting her thumb at him)*

SANCHO

Oh, is that so? *(To Don Quixote)* Wait, señor, don't leave. *(Softly)* That little old lady just bit her thumb at me.

QUIXOTE

You're lying, scoundrel!

SANCHO

I'm telling you the truth, señor. What do you want me to do—let an insult go unanswered?

QUIXOTE

Do you want my head to roll, brigand?

DUKE

What is it, Señor Don Quixote?

QUIXOTE

Ah, Your Grace, don't listen to him!

SANCHO

No, why shouldn't he know? *(To Duke)* She bit her thumb at me. *(Does the same to Duke)*

DUKE

Rodriguez? Yes, she has a nasty personality. Well, so do it back to her.

SANCHO

Right. Thank you.

QUIXOTE

Your Grace! . . .

DUKE

Enough of this, enough, let's go and wash up, Señor Don Quixote.

They exit.

SANCHO

(To Rodriguez) And the same to you!

He gives it back to her.

RODRIGUEZ

Ah! . . . Ah! . . . Ah! . . .

She runs off. Sancho exits following Don Quixote.
   Music. Servants bring wine. After a while, Don Quixote, Duchess and Duke return and sit down at the table. Sancho installs himself behind Don Quixote's chair. Duke's Confessor enters and seats himself to one side.

DUCHESS

Tell us, Don Quixote, how long is it since you've had news of the lovely, enchanted Dulcinea del Toboso?

QUIXOTE

Most gracious señora, my misfortunes are without end! I have defeated more than one giant already and sent them all to kneel before her, but they cannot find her, because the evil magic powers have turned her into an ugly, simple peasant woman.

DUKE

How very sad.

CONFESSOR

What's this I hear? *(To Duke)* Your Grace, you will have to answer for this at the Last Judgment. By encouraging these two mad-men, you lead everyone into temptation. *(To Don Quixote)* And you? How did you get it into your head that you're a knight errant defeating giants and taking them captive? Stop wandering about the world, drinking the wind, and making yourself a laughing-stock. Stop this raving, go home, educate your children if you have any, and look after your property! Where in Spain have you ever seen knights errant, giants, and enchanted princesses? Where are they? Don't you see people are laughing at you?

DUKE

Wait a minute, Reverend Father! . . .

DUCHESS

Reverend Father, please! . . .

QUIXOTE

No, Your Grace, allow me to answer! *(To Confessor)* Bear in mind that it is only the fact that I am the Duke's guest and you are a priest that holds back my fury, otherwise it would go badly for you. So, then, I'll fight you with your own weapon—my tongue. Tell me, for precisely which of my ravings do you condemn me most of all, telling me to go home and teach the children I've never had? You think that a man who wanders through the world not in search of pleasures but of thorns is mad and idly wasting his time? People choose different paths. One man, stumbling, climbs the path of vainglory, another crawls down the road of humiliating flattery, still others choose the way of hypocrisy and deceit. Do I follow any of these roads? No! I follow the steep path of chivalry, and scorn worldly goods, but not honor! Whom have I avenged by struggling against the giants who annoy you so much? I have defended the weak, those who are insulted by the strong! Seeing evil anywhere, I entered into mortal combat to defeat the monsters of malice and crime! You don't see them anywhere? Then you have poor eyesight, Reverend Father. My goal is bright: to do good for everyone, and to cause no one evil. And for that, in your opinion, I am worthy of reproach? If it were a knight who considered me mad, I would be deeply offended, but your words aren't worth a cent, I find them ridiculous!

SANCHO

Beautifully put, I swear by the governorship my master is going to win for me.

CONFESSOR

(To Sancho) Come to your senses, you pitiful madman! What governorship are you dreaming of, you dim-witted ignoramus?

SANCHO

(Softly, to Don Quixote) Señor, he's calling me names!

DUKE

Oh, no, no, here you're mistaken, Reverend Father. Right now, in front of everybody, I announce that I am appointing the squire Sancho Panza governor of the island of Barataria, which is part of the lands belonging to me.

DUCHESS

I'm delighted with your decision, Duke!

SANCHO

(To Confessor) So I'm a dim-witted ignoramus! Ah, what a pity my wife Juana Teresa isn't here, she'd drop dead from joy!

QUIXOTE

Sancho, thank the most gracious Duke for fulfilling your cherished dream.

CONFESSOR

Your Grace, you are making as much sense as they are! But as it's not in my power to get you to stop all this, I'd rather not waste my breath, I'll leave you! *(Exits)*

DUCHESS

(To Don Quixote) You answered the confessor very well, señor. Everyone could see that his wrath was unjustified.

DUKE

Indeed. Now go to your island, Sancho, where the people there are awaiting you like spring rain.

QUIXOTE

Allow me to give him a few admonitions, Your Grace, to help him guard against false steps in his new and exalted position.

DUKE

That's a very good idea, señor.

DUCHESS

We will withdraw and leave you two alone.

Everyone exits except Don Quixote and Sancho.

QUIXOTE

Listen to me carefully, Sancho. I'm moved, my heart is stirred. You have suddenly obtained something for which some people make incredible efforts, driven by ambition or greed, resorting to various, often shady, means, and still do not always achieve what they want. I tell you this so that you will not ascribe the luck that has befallen you to your own merits and puff yourself up like a frog, so that you may avoid the mockery and possibly also the wicked slander from which no position, however exalted, is safe. Be proud that you are a simple peasant, Sancho. Do not consider it humiliating to acknowledge it to anyone. There's no need to prove to you that a poor but honest man is worth more than a noble sinner and scoundrel. Do not reject your origin or your family. What else did I want to say? Ah, yes! You will have to mete out justice to people. That is difficult, Sancho! Listen to me, and don't forget a word I say. When you mete out justice, do not be arbitrary. Will you remember that?

SANCHO

I will, señor.

QUIXOTE

Seek the truth tirelessly everywhere, and let the tears of a poor man affect you more than the assurances of a rich one—and more especially his promises. Be guided by the law, but remember: if the law is strict, do not try to crush the condemned with its full weight. Know that the fame of a strict judge is never greater than that of a merciful one. Anything can happen at a trial. For instance, you may find your enemy facing you. What do you do in that case? Forget the personal offence at once, and judge him as if you were seeing him for the first time in your life. There are occasions, Sancho, when the rod of justice trembles in a judge's hand. If that happens to you, do not lower it because someone whispers in your ear and puts a jingling purse in your pocket! Remember this last thing especially, Sancho, if you don't want me to despise you. And if, out of faintheartedness, you ever do lower your rod of justice, let it be from compassion alone! What else shall I tell you? Never be rude to your subordinates, Sancho, and, I beg you, stop your babbling! Know that babbling can lead you to the gallows, and . . . wash your face! If you follow this advice, you'll be happy in your new position. Have you understood me? Have you?

SANCHO

You needn't worry any more, señor, I understand you.

QUIXOTE

Look me in the eye. Yes, I believe you. Well, then, let's say our farewells. We won't be seeing each other again: our ways have parted.

I'll rest here in the Duke's castle, and then set out for wherever
duty takes me.

SANCHO

Ah, sir ...

QUIXOTE

What are you sighing for?

SANCHO

I'm thinking—what will you do without a squire.

QUIXOTE

I'll find somebody else.

SANCHO

Will anybody go with you, that's the question! You know, señor,
I suggest that you promise him an island, too. I'd stay with you,
but ...

QUIXOTE

No, no, I understand very well.

SANCHO

Allow me, señor, to give you a little advice, too, before I go. What
did I want to tell you? Ah, yes. I feel in my heart that sooner or
later you're going to get beaten up, señor. So, in a fight, protect
your head first and foremost, don't let them hit your head. It's full
of intelligent thoughts, and it would be a shame if it got smashed
like a clay pot. Let your ribs take the hits—one or two ribs—that's
no great loss! ... What else, señor? Ah, yes. You have one bottle
of that Fierabras elixir left. Pour it out, señor, and to hell with it,
because if the beatings don't finish you off, that elixir will. Do as
I tell you—and you'll be happy in your new position! And I'm
going to miss you very much.

QUIXOTE

I thank you for your concern for me. Farewell and fare forward!

Trumpets sound, the doors open wide. Enter Duchess, Duke and pages with a governor's uniform.

Scene 3

A hall in Duke's country seat. A judge's chair. A bed under a canopy. Trumpets. Sancho, in the governor's uniform, enters with his suite and sits down.

MAJORDOMO

Señor Governor, there is an ancient custom on our island of Barataria that a new governor, on entering office, should publicly decide two or three puzzling cases, so that the populace can find out whether the new governor is intelligent or an utter and irrevocable idiot, and, depending on that, can know whether to rejoice—or despair.

SANCHO

Bring on your cases!

MAJORDOMO

Yes, Your Honor!

Enter two elderly litigants. One is carrying a cane.

SANCHO

What is your problem, my friends?

FIRST OLD MAN

I lent him ten gold pieces, Your Honor, and when he was supposed to pay me back, I asked him for the money and he said he already gave it to me. In fact, that's not true, but I have no witnesses. And however many courts I go to, I can't do anything about it, because he swears he gave me back the money. Help me, Señor Governor!

SANCHO

(To Second Old Man) Did he give you ten gold pieces?

SECOND OLD MAN

He did, Your Honor, he did, but I gave them back.

FIRST OLD MAN

He's lying, Your Honor, he never gave them back!

SECOND OLD MAN

No, *he's* lying, I gave him back everything I owed.

SANCHO

(To Second Old Man) And you're ready to swear to that?

SECOND OLD MAN

Anytime.

SANCHO

All right, swear.

SECOND OLD MAN

(To First Old Man) Would you mind holding my cane, neighbor?

First Old Man takes his cane. Second Old Man takes hold of Sancho's staff.

I solemnly swear that I've given back the ten gold pieces he lent me.

FIRST OLD MAN

Oh, why doesn't God punish him!

Second Old Man reaches for his cane.

SANCHO

No, friend, you've told the truth, but let him keep the cane.

FIRST OLD MAN

Is it worth ten gold pieces, Your Honor?

SANCHO

It is! It is, or I've got bricks in my head in place of brains. Break open the cane!

They break open the cane, and money rolls out of it.

FIRST OLD MAN

My money! Oh, wisest of all governors!

SECOND OLD MAN

(Falling to his knees) Forgive me, Señor Governor!

SANCHO

Get out, you wily swindler! But remember, if you take it into your head to trick somebody again, I won't be so easy on you.

FIRST OLD MAN

Oh, Great Governor!

MAJORDOMO AND SUITE

Great Governor!

The old men exit.
Enter Woman and Pig Farmer.

WOMAN

Justice! Justice! If I'm denied it here on earth, I'll seek it in Heaven!

SANCHO

What has happened to you, my dear?

WOMAN

Your Honor, this bastard met me in the fields today and forced himself on me!

SANCHO

(To Pig Farmer) Ah-ha, I see, so you're a . . .

PIG FARMER

(Despairingly) I'm a pig farmer, Your Honor . . .

SANCHO

Well, so you're a pig farmer . . . Nothing follows from that, my friend . . . there's no . . .

PIG FARMER

All I mean, Your Honor, is that I really did meet her in the fields today . . . You see, I sold four pigs today . . . and . . . in fact, there was a bit of mischief . . . but she agreed . . . and I even paid her.

WOMAN

He's lying!

SANCHO

Well, my dear pig farmer, have you got any money on you?

PIG FARMER

Yes, I have, Your Honor. Twenty silver ducats.

SANCHO

Pay up, then, my friend.

Pig Farmer, in despair, hands his purse to Woman.

WOMAN

May the Lord grant long life to our governor, the protector of all the oppressed! *(Exits)*

SANCHO

(To Pig Farmer) Why are you so upset, friend?

PIG FARMER

I'm sorry to lose my money!

SANCHO

Well, in that case go and take your purse back from her.

Pig Farmer rushes out. Screams are heard, then Woman runs in, dragging Pig Farmer behind her.

WOMAN

Señor Governor! This robber, in broad daylight, tried to take back the purse you ordered him to give me.

SANCHO

And did he succeed?

WOMAN

I'd sooner part with my soul than with this money! Even with a lion's claws he won't tear it away from me.

PIG FARMER

She can have the money!

SANCHO

(To Woman) Give me the purse.

WOMAN

What is it, Señor Governor?

SANCHO

Give me the purse now! If you had defended your honor as force-
fully as you did this money, even Hercules couldn't have taken it from
you! Get out, you greedy liar! *(To Pig Farmer)* Here's your purse.

PIG FARMER

Thank you, good Señor Governor.

SANCHO

Well, all right, all right, go now, and in the future don't be so careless.

PIG FARMER

(Leaving) Long live our governor!

MAJORDOMO

The people are delighted with you, Señor Governor! The cases
are closed, and supper is ready.

SANCHO

Then I'm delighted, too. Bring it on!

*A sumptuously laid table appears. Sancho sits down. Doctor Aguero
appears behind Sancho's chair. As soon as Sancho touches some one
of the dishes, Doctor Aguero points to it with his staff, and the plate
is taken away.*

What are you doing?

AGUERO

Señor Governor, I am a doctor, especially appointed to attend to
your person and watch out lest you eat something that might be
bad for your precious health. That dish is bad for you.

SANCHO

Then give me the partridge!

AGUERO

No, no, no! Hippocrates, the father of medicine and teacher of all doctors, says that . . .

SANCHO

All right, all right, if he says so. What about rabbit?!

AGUERO

You can't be serious, Señor Governor!

SANCHO

May I ask what your name is and where you studied?

AGUERO

I am Doctor Pedro Recio de Aguero, born in a village between Caracuel and Almodóvar del Campo, and I was granted my doctoral degree by the University of Osuna.

SANCHO

I tell you what, my dear Doctor Pedro Recio de Aguero, born in Almodóvar del Campo! Get the hell out of here, and take that degree granted you by the University of Osuna with you! Out!

AGUERO

Señor Governor!

SANCHO

Out!

Doctor Aguero runs out.

Give me the rabbit!

MAJORDOMO

Yes, Señor Governor.

Sancho begins to eat. Trumpets sound. Majordomo hands Sancho a letter.

A letter to Your Honor from the Duke.

SANCHO

Who is my secretary here?

MAJORDOMO

I am, Your Honor.

SANCHO

Can you read?

MAJORDOMO

But of course, Your Honor!

SANCHO

Read it, even if it's word by word. I'll figure it out.

MAJORDOMO

(Reads) "Dear Governor, information has reached me that enemies plan to attack the island entrusted to you one of these nights. Take appropriate measures . . ."

SANCHO

Forget the rabbit. I've lost my appetite. *(To Majordomo)* Thanks a lot for that. I'm genuinely sorry you learned how to read.

MAJORDOMO

There's a bit more.

SANCHO

Okay, finish me off.

MAJORDOMO

(Reads) "Besides that, I must inform you, dear Governor, that your enemies are going to make attempts on your life. Be careful at mealtimes, you may be poisoned. Yours truly, the Duke."

SANCHO

Somehow I knew it would just get better and better. Clear this table away right now! Clear it all away! *(He gets up)* My God, my God! If I can't eat, at last let me sleep in peace after all my hard work.

MAJORDOMO

Yes, Señor Governor!

The lights dim. Sancho is taken to his bed and disappears behind the canopy.
The table is removed. The hall is empty. Soft music. Then an alarm bell, noise in the distance.
Sancho peeks from behind the canopy.

SANCHO

What's that?

There is a gunshot in the distance.

Ah, that's it, what's written in that damn letter, it's coming true!

He disappears behind the canopy.

MAJORDOMO

(Runs in carrying a sword) Señor Governor! Señor Governor!

SANCHO

(Peeking out) What is it? I hope everything on the island is in order?

MAJORDOMO

No, sir! Enemies are attacking! To arms! To arms! Stand at the head of our army, otherwise we'll all be slaughtered like chickens!

SANCHO

To arms? Oh, if only my master was here! Just my luck!

He disappears behind the canopy.

MAJORDOMO

(Drawing the canopy aside) Your Honor, what's taking you so long?

SUITE

(Bursting in with torches) To arms!

MAJORDOMO

Bring the big shields!

Sancho is packed between two enormous shields, so that he now resembles a huge turtle.

Forward, Señor Governor, forward!

SANCHO

What do you mean, forward? I can't even move!

MAJORDOMO

Lift up the governor!

Sancho is lifted up and carried out. Noise of battle, flashing torch-light. The shields come rolling back onstage. Sancho lies helplessly between them, his head drawn in. His suite loudly stomps around him. Outside the windows, shouts and gunshots.
    Majordomo jumps on Sancho's upper shield, commands:

Forward, islanders, forward! Where's the boiling oil? Good! Pour it on them! Throw them off the ladders! Forward! Forward! Ah, they're wavering! Bandage the wounded! Here! To me!

He dances on the shield.

SUITE

(Variously) The enemy's wavering! They're running away! Victory! Victory! . . .

The "fighting" dies down.

MAJORDOMO

(Jumps off the shield) Victory! Unpack the governor!

Sancho is unpacked and set on his feet.

I congratulate you, Your Honor. The army of the island, under your command, has repelled the enemy! You can celebrate!

SANCHO

I need a drink.

They bring Sancho wine.

No, forget it. Maybe your wine is poisoned, too, eh? Forget it. Bring me my donkey.

MAJORDOMO

Yes, Señor Governor.

SANCHO

Let me through, señores.

The suite step aside, and Sancho disappears behind the canopy. The donkey is brought to the terrace beyond the hall. Sancho comes from behind the canopy dressed in his usual clothes.

Come to me, my donkey! Come to me, my faithful gray friend!

He embraces the donkey.

We used to live for each other once: you for me, and me for you. Back then our only care was to keep your little body fed. How happy we were then, both at home and wandering. But now, having achieved the height of ambition, a thousand troubles, two thousand sorrows torment my body and soul! Make way, señores! I'll return to my old life. I'll go back to my knight. I wasn't born to be a governor. I know how to prune grapevines, but not how to govern islands. I'm used to holding a sickle, and prefer it to a governor's staff. I sleep more peacefully on the grass than in a governor's finest sheets, and I feel warmer in my jacket than in a governor's coat. Good-bye, señores, good-bye! But tell the Duke that I left as poor as I came. I've lost nothing, and I've gained nothing. See, my pockets are empty, I haven't stolen a thing. Good-bye!

He gets on his donkey.

MAJORDOMO

Señor Governor, please stay with us!

SUITE

Stay with us!

SANCHO

Oh, no, not for anything in the world! My soul is as beaten and broken as my body is.

AGUERO

Señor Governor, I'll give you the best plasters and medicines!

SANCHO

Oh, no! No plasters of yours will draw the stubbornness out of me! I'm a Sancho, once I've decided, I stick to it!

MAJORDOMO

We've come to love you, Governor, for your intelligence and wisdom! Stay with us!

SANCHO

No, no, make way!

MAJORDOMO

Well, there's nothing we can do! Good-bye, Sancho Panza! You were the best and most honest governor who ever ruled this island! Good-bye!

SANCHO

Good-bye!

He rides off.
    Curtain.

ACT FIVE

Scene 1

Duke's terrace and garden. The garden is lit up. Music. Duke and Duchess are sitting on the terrace.

QUIXOTE

(Offstage) "Oh, jealousy, cruel ruler of the land of love, put fetters on my arms . . ."

DUCHESS

Another fit of raving. Do you hear how he's shouting verses to the music? I feel sorry for him. I think if it weren't for this unfortunate madness, he'd be one of the most intelligent men I've ever known. When his visions lift, he makes perfect sense, his thoughts are clear.

DUKE

You're mistaken, my dear, he's incurable. And the only thing left to hope for is that his madness at least entertains people.

Trumpets sound. Enter Page.

PAGE

Your Grace, some knight has come to the castle and is asking to be received.

DUKE

What knight?

PAGE

Nobody knows him. He's wearing armor and his visor is down.

DUKE

Ah, you pages! This is the majordomo's joke!

PAGE

No, it's not, Your Grace, really! Nobody knows the man, and he refuses to give his name!

DUKE

Well, all right, all right, in any case it's amusing. Ask him to come here.

Page exits. Trumpets sound. Enter Sansón dressed in armor and carrying a sword and shield. On his breastplate is a picture of the moon.

SANSÓN

Forgive me, Your Grace, for coming to your castle uninvited.

DUKE

I'm very glad. Who are you?

SANSÓN

I am the Knight of the White Moon.

DUKE

Ah, that's very interesting! *(To Duchess)* So now we've got two madmen in the castle. *(To Sansón)* What brings you here, knight? Though I'm glad to see you, whatever the reason.

SANSÓN

I have been told that Don Quixote is your guest here. I have come to see him.

DUKE

Yes, Don Quixote is here with us, and I'll be glad to give you the opportunity of seeing each other. *(To Page)* Ask Don Quixote to come here.

PAGE

Yes, sir.

Page exits.

DUCHESS

I'm feeling slightly uneasy, Duke. You're sure it's safe to do this?

DUKE

Don't worry, dear, I promise you this is someone's idea of a joke.

QUIXOTE

(Declaiming offstage) Yes, my death is at hand . . . I'm dying. And I no longer hope for anything either in life or in death! . . .

He enters dressed in armor but without a helmet, sees Sansón.

Who is this? *(To Duke)* Ah, Your Grace! Why don't you invite your confessor here? It was he who said there were no more knights or monsters in Spain! This would convince him that knights errant exist. Besides me, here is a second one standing before you! Here is a second one! You see, his armor flashes like fire and warlike valor blazes in his eyes—I can see them through the slits in his visor! So, why have I been summoned here?

SANSÓN

I have come to see you, Don Quixote de la Mancha.

QUIXOTE

Here I am.

SANSÓN

Don Quixote! I am called the Knight of the White Moon.

QUIXOTE

What brings you to me?

SANSÓN

I have come to throw down a challenge to you, Don Quixote! I will force you to acknowledge that my lady, whatever she's called, is more beautiful than your Dulcinea del Toboso! And if you do not acknowledge it, you will have to fight me. One of us will be defeated and will obey the orders of the victor. I await your reply.

QUIXOTE

Knight of the White Moon, I have never read or heard of your exploits and so cannot be impressed by them, but I am impressed by your arrogance. Undoubtedly you have never seen Dulcinea del Toboso. Otherwise you would not have dared to speak of her that way!

SANSÓN

I dare to speak of her as I like, since I am challenging you! Answer me: do you or do you not accept my challenge?

QUIXOTE

Enough, Knight of the White Moon, your challenge is accepted. *(To Page)* Give me my helmet and shield! Duke, divide the daylight between us!

DUCHESS

They're going to fight? I'm frightened!

DUKE

Come now, Duchess, it's extremely interesting! Ho, there, bring torches!

Torches are brought. Page hands Don Quixote the barber's basin and the shield.

Where do you want to stand, Knight of the White Moon?

SANSÓN

Right where I am.

DUKE

Stand here, Don Quixote.

QUIXOTE

My lady, help the one of us who is right!

DUKE

Advance.

Don Quixote rushes at Sansón and manages to strike him with his sword. Sansón's left arm hangs limp.

SANSÓN

Ahh!

He attacks Don Quixote, furiously breaks his sword, smashes his shield and breastplate, and knocks the barber's basin off his head. Don Quixote falls.

DUCHESS

That's enough! That's enough! He's beaten!

DUKE

Stop!

SANSÓN

No, step back, all of you! I have my own accounts to settle with him!

He puts the point of his sword to Don Quixote's throat.

Surrender, Knight of the Mournful Countenance, you are defeated. Fulfill the conditions of the fight and repeat after me: Yes, Knight of the White Moon, your lady is more beautiful than Dulcinea. Repeat it!

QUIXOTE

Yes, your lady . . . No, I can't! I'm defeated, I'm defeated, I admit it . . . but I cannot agree that there is anything in the world more beautiful than Dulcinea! There is no woman more beautiful! But something suddenly frightens me much more than the point of your sword! It's your eyes! . . . Your gaze is cold and cruel, and I've suddenly begun to imagine that Dulcinea doesn't exist! No, she doesn't! . . . My brow is bathed in cold sweat at the thought! She doesn't exist! . . . But even so I won't utter the words you are trying to tear out of me. There is no woman more beautiful! But your heart of iron cannot understand that! Stab me, I have no fear of death!

SANSÓN

I will kill you!

DUKE

Stop, I order you!

Sancho enters.

SANCHO

Señor Don Quixote! . . . My dear señor . . . I've come just in time
. . . I ran away from the island, I'm not a governor anymore! Listen
to your squire's advice—admit you're defeated! *(To Duke)* Your
Grace, don't let the most honorable and wise hidalgo be robbed
of his life!

DUCHESS

Stop fighting! I won't allow this . . .

SANSÓN

I repeat again—let us be! *(To Don Quixote)* I'll accept that. Live
with your dream of Dulcinea—she doesn't exist. I'm satisfied: my
lady does exist, and that already makes her more beautiful than
yours! Repeat after me: At the request of the Knight of the White
Moon, who has defeated me, I am ready to withdraw to my estate
in La Mancha forever, to perform no further exploits, and to go
nowhere anymore.

QUIXOTE

Heart of stone . . .

SANSÓN

Go on, swear! Before I lose my patience!

DUCHESS

Swear!

SANCHO

Swear!

QUIXOTE

I swear . . . I'm defeated . . .

Sansón sheaths his sword and steps aside.

Who's here with me? . . . Sancho . . . Help me, Sancho, my collarbone is broken.

SANCHO

Help me lift him up!

Pages rush to Don Quixote and lift him up.

DUCHESS

Send for the doctor!

Don Quixote is carried off. Duke and Sansón remain onstage.

DUKE

This joke has gone too far, and now I demand you raise that visor and tell me who you are.

SANSÓN

(Raising his visor) I'm the scholar Sansón Carrasco from La Mancha, I've never been a knight and don't want to be one. I felt sorry for the poor hidalgo Alonso Quixano. I respect him and love him, and I decided to put an end to his ravings and sufferings.

DUKE

Hm . . . That is a good deed, scholar, and I see you've paid for it with your arm. Well, the more honor to you! But all the same I can't help regretting that Quixano's adventures are over. They were amusing, and he and his squire were entertaining people.

SANSÓN

Let's not be sorry about that, Your Grace. As if there weren't enough entertainments in the world! Hunting, dances by torchlight, banquets and jousts ... The rich don't lack for that. So why do you need to entertain yourselves by adding to the already large number of buffoons and making a buffoon of a man who doesn't deserve it in the least?

DUKE

Do I catch a whiff of moralizing in your words, my dear scholar? I am not at all accustomed to that.

SANSÓN

Heaven forbid, Duke! I'm not so bold as to dare tell you what to do. I was just thinking out loud.

DUKE

Then a little advice, scholar: if you're going to think out loud, do it in your own home. If I had known what you were up to, I'd never have let you in.

SANSÓN

Oh, I guessed that would be the case, so I got in by pretending to be part of the entertainment, wishing only to please your Grace.

DUKE

Enough! Good-bye!

Sansón turns and exits.

Ho, there! Show the Knight of the White Moon out of the castle!

Trumpets.

Scene 2

*Courtyard of Don Quixote's house. Sunset. The rooms and court-
yard are empty. On the road going downhill, outside the gate, Don
Quixote and Sancho appear. Don Quixote is stooping and leaning
on a stick; one arm is in a sling. Sancho is leading Rocinante and
the donkey. Rocinante is heaped with armor in such a way that it
looks like an empty knight on horseback with a broken lance.*

SANCHO
Here's our village, señor! Oh, my longed-for motherland! Behold
your son, Sancho Panza. Open your arms to him. He comes back
to you undistinguished, but very rich in experience, gained from
calamities, anxieties, and a lot of bad luck. He's gone through
everything, from a rain of sticks pouring down on his miserable, helpless body, from people who jeered, mocked, and had
no understanding of what a knight's squire is, to the unheard-of
honors that fell on his head when he became a governor! And
now that governorship has vanished like smoke, the pain of the
blows is gone, and the son of his motherland comes back to
where he started from—under the shade of these trees, to his famil-
iar well!

*He tethers Rocinante and the donkey. Meanwhile, Don Quixote
stands motionless on the hill above the courtyard, gazing into the
distance.*

Niece! Señora housekeeper! I'm not afraid to fill the air with my
shouting, because I know that you, señora housekeeper, will not
grab me in your sharp claws or shower me with abuse that turns
the bravest hearts cold. We've come back for good! Today's Satur-
day, she's in church . . . Señor Don Quixote, why don't you come
in? What are you looking at, señor?

QUIXOTE

The sun. There it is, the eye of Heaven, the eternal torch of the universe, the creator of music and the healer of men! But the day declines towards evening and an irresistible power pulls it down. A little while longer and it will go under the earth. Then it will be dark. But the darkness won't last, Sancho! In a few hours light will shine from over the edge of the earth, and again the chariot no man can look at will rise into the sky. And I've been thinking, Sancho, that when the chariot I've been riding in begins to go down under the earth, it won't rise again. When my day ends, Sancho, there will be no other. Anguish comes over me at the thought of it, because I feel that my only day is ending.

SANCHO

Don't scare me, señor! Your wounds have opened. Everybody knows when the body aches, the soul does too. You're ill, sir, you must go right to bed.

Don Quixote comes into the courtyard and sits down on a bench.

Let's go, sir, I'll put you to bed, they'll give you a bite to eat, and sleep will heal you.

QUIXOTE

No! I want to look at the trees . . . See, the leaves are yellow . . . Yes, Sancho, the day is coming to an end, it's clear. I'm afraid, because I am meeting my sunset quite empty, and there's nothing to fill that emptiness.

SANCHO

What emptiness, señor? I don't understand this sadness, and these complicated thoughts. Though as a governor I was pretty sharp. That damn Knight of the White Moon—may he be squashed in his first battle like an overripe melon!—could he and his sword have hurt not just your body but your immortal soul?

QUIXOTE

Ah, Sancho, Sancho! The damage done me by his steel is insignificant. Nor did he cripple my soul with his strokes. My fear is that he has cured my soul, and, having cured it, has taken it out of me without replacing it with another . . . He has deprived me of the most precious gift a man is endowed with—he has deprived me of my freedom! There is much evil in the world, Sancho, but no evil is worse than captivity! He has put me in chains, Sancho! . . . Look, the sun is cut in half, the earth is rising higher and higher, devouring it. The earth is closing over the prisoner! It will engulf me, Sancho!

SANCHO

Ah, sir, the more you say, the less I understand. All I can see is that you're suffering, and I don't know how to help you! How can I cheer you up? Where's my former knight? Well, all right, he defeated you, and you're not going to wander and draw your sword anymore. But remember, sir, you said if worst came to worst you'd be a shepherd! I'll gladly go with you, sir, if you give me another couple of donkeys, because I've gotten very used to you . . . Say something, sir. Ah, fate itself is coming to help me! Now I'll see how your eyes blaze with fire. Stand up, sir, your dream is coming, Dulcinea del Toboso is coming to you!

Through the gate leading to the village, Aldonza Lorenzo enters with a basket. On seeing Don Quixote, she gets frightened.

ALDONZA

Oh, not again! Here's that crazy hidalgo right in my way!

SANCHO

Princess of beauty and queen of majesty! Your obedient knight Don Quixote de la Mancha stands before you!

ALDONZA

So now you've lost your mind, too, fat Sancho Panza? Or are you just making fun of me? If that's it, save your jokes for somebody else. Leave me alone. And stop calling me Dulcinea! Aldonza I've been and Aldonza I'll stay! Everybody laughs at me as it is, because of your master, poor man. Give this basket to the housekeeper, and let me go!

SANCHO

Don't listen to her, señor, she's still enchanted.

QUIXOTE

Aldonza!

ALDONZA

What is it, sir?

QUIXOTE

Are you afraid of me?

ALDONZA

Yes, I am. You talk strange, sir, and you don't know who people are . . .

QUIXOTE

I'll tell you who you are. You're Aldonza Lorenzo, a peasant girl from the next village. You've never been Dulcinea del Toboso. I called you that, but my mind was darkened, and I ask you to forgive me for it. Well, are you afraid of me now?

ALDONZA

No, sir. So you really know who I am?

QUIXOTE

I do, Aldonza . . . Go in peace, we won't offend you. Don't keep her, Sancho.

Aldonza runs off.

SANCHO

Well, sir, now I can see that the White Moon has turned everything upside down in your head! Hang me if I don't keep thinking I see that knight everywhere . . . as we were getting close to the village, I even imagined I saw him sneaking along after us through the fields.

QUIXOTE

You didn't imagine it, Sancho, it was really so. He was following us through the fields, though he's not a knight and never has been. No, he's not a knight, and yet he's the best knight of all we met during our wanderings. But he's a cruel knight.

SANCHO

I swear even the best of governors won't understand that riddle!

QUIXOTE

Let's go in.

They go in, Sancho carrying the armor. In the room, Sancho puts the armor in the corner and draws the bed canopy aside.

SANCHO

Oh, now I see how ill you are, sir! Lie down at once, and I'll run and get the priest and the barber. They'll help you. I'll be right back, sir.

He runs out to the courtyard and exits, leading his donkey.
After a while, Antonia appears, comes into the courtyard. On the hill outside the gate, the figure of Sansón emerges, dressed in armor. Sansón walks slowly, and his arm, like Don Quixote's, is in a sling.

ANTONIA

Oh my God! Who is this? My uncle? No, it's not him! Have I myself gone mad from grief? Is this a knight I see in the sunset, or is the setting sun playing tricks on me? There's a moon shining on his chest and feathers waving on his helmet! Are we all mad, and my uncle's the only sane one? Was he right when he said that knights errant exist? . . . Who are you?

SANSÓN

(Entering) It's me, Antonia.

He takes his helmet off.

ANTONIA

Sansón!

SANSÓN

Careful, Antonia, my arm is hurt.

ANTONIA

Are you wounded, Sansón? What happened to you?

SANSÓN

No, no. *(Freeing himself of the armor)* May that shield with the moon go to hell, and take the sword along with it!

ANTONIA

Sansón, you said you'd come back only if . . . Where is my uncle? Is he alive?

SANSÓN

(Pointing to the house) He's at home. I've kept my word, Antonia, and Alonso Quixano will never leave again.

ANTONIA

At home? . . . At home? If that's so, Sansón, you're a real magician. No wonder you're a scholar! Of course you're a scholar, you're the smartest man in the world! Ah, what am I saying! . . . I'm getting confused . . . Because I'm happy, Sansón! How did you do it? Sansón! Sansón!

She kisses him.

SANSÓN

How can you kiss a coward and a deceiver?

ANTONIA

Stop that, Sansón! You're being mean! Why are you throwing that back in my face? I was upset, grieving then, I didn't mean what I said. No, no, Sansón, you're our best friend, you're a wonderful and noble man!

She kisses Sansón and runs into the house. The sun has gone down, and it turns dark.

Uncle! Where are you?

QUIXOTE

(Behind the canopy) Who's there?

ANTONIA

It's me, Señor Alonso, me, Antonia!

She pulls the canopy aside.

QUIXOTE

I feel like I'm suffocating, Antonia . . .

ANTONIA

Lie down! Lie down right now!

QUIXOTE

No, no, I'm suffocating . . . and uneasy . . . I'd better sit here . . . call somebody, Antonia, call somebody!

ANTONIA

The scholar Carrasco is here, Uncle, shall I get him?

QUIXOTE

Ah, he's come? I was expecting that. Call him here, but be quick about it.

ANTONIA

Sansón! Sansón!

SANSÓN

I'm here, Señor Don Quixote!

QUIXOTE

Why do you call me that? You realize perfectly well that I'm not Don Quixote de la Mancha, but the same old Alonso Quixano, called the Good, just as you are the scholar Sansón Carrasco and not the Knight of the White Moon.

SANSÓN

So you know everything?

QUIXOTE

Yes. I recognized your eyes behind the visor and that voice mercilessly demanding obedience . . . then, at our combat. My reason was freed of dark shadows. It happened to me then, when you, Sansón, stood over me in the bloody light of torches in the castle . . . In short, I see you now, I see everything.

SANSÓN

Forgive me, Señor Quixano, for fighting you!

QUIXOTE

No, no, I'm grateful to you. With your strokes, you brought me out of the prison of madness. But I regret that this reasonableness cannot be prolonged. Has the sun set, Antonia? . . . Here he is! . . .

ANTONIA

Señor Alonso, calm down! There's no one here!

QUIXOTE

No, no, don't comfort me, Antonia, my daughter, I'm not afraid. I've anticipated it and expected him since morning. And now he's come for me. I'm glad of it. When Sansón frightened off the string of hateful figures that tormented me when my mind was darkened, I was afraid I would be left in emptiness. But now he has come and is filling my empty armor, and is twining around me in the darkness . . .

SANSÓN

Wine, Antonia, bring him wine! . . .

QUIXOTE

Antonia . . . marry someone who was never carried away by reading about knights, but who has the soul of a knight . . . Sansón, you have a lady, and this lady truly is more beautiful than Dulcinea. She is alive, your lady . . . Call the housekeeper . . . No, no—Sancho! . . . Bring me Sancho! Sancho! . . .

He falls. Sancho comes running across the courtyard and into the house.

SANCHO

Señor scholar! Help him!

SANSÓN

Antonia, give him wine! Sancho, bring a light!

Antonia runs out.

SANCHO

Señor Quixano! Don't die! Señor Don Quixote, do you recognize my voice? Look at me! It's me, Sancho! . . . We'll become shepherds, I'll go with you! . . . Why don't you answer me? . . .

Antonia runs in with a lamp.

ANTONIA

What should we do, Sansón? What should we do?

SANCHO

He doesn't answer me!

SANSÓN

There's nothing more I can do. He's dead.

CURTAIN

MIKHAIL BULGAKOV was born in Kiev on May 15, 1891. He studied medicine and began to practice in his native city just as the Revolution and Civil War overtook Russia. After some wanderings in eastern provinces, he decided to abandon medicine and in 1921 settled permanently in Moscow, where he pursued his literary career. During the early twenties he wrote journalism, plays, stories, and the novel *The White Guard*, which, turned into the play *Days of the Turbins*, premiered at the famous Moscow Art Theatre in 1926. He continued to write plays for the Art Theatre and other theaters, but came under severe criticism from official revolutionary circles and was able to publish and produce very little during the last decade of his life. Among his unpublished works were his fine *Life of Monsieur de Molière* and his great novel, *The Master and Margarita*, both of which appeared for the first time more than two decades after his death on March 10, 1940.

RICHARD NELSON's plays include the four-play series *The Apple Family: Scenes from Life in the Country* (*That Hopey Changey Thing*, *Sweet and Sad*, *Sorry* and *Regular Singing*), *Nikolai and the Others*, *Farewell to the Theatre*, *Conversations in Tusculum*, *How Shakespeare Won the West*, *Frank's Home*, *Rodney's Wife*, *Franny's Way*, *Madame Melville*, *Goodnight Children Everywhere*, *New England*, *The General from America*, *Misha's Party* (with Alexander Gelman), *Two Shakespearean Actors* and *Some Americans Abroad*. He has written the musicals *James Joyce's The Dead* (with Shaun Davey) and *My Life with Albertine* (with Ricky Ian Gordon), and the screenplays for the films *Hyde Park-on-Hudson* and *Ethan Frome*. He has received numerous awards, including a Tony (Best Book of a Musical for *James Joyce's The Dead*), an Olivier (Best Play for *Goodnight Children Everywhere*) and two New York Drama Critics' Circle Awards (*James Joyce's The Dead* and *The Apple Family*). He is the recipient of the PEN/Laura Pels Master Playwright Award, an Academy Award from the American Academy of Arts and Letters; he is an Honorary Associate Artist of the Royal Shakespeare Company. He lives in upstate New York.

RICHARD PEVEAR was born in Boston, grew up on Long Island, attended Allegheny College (BA 1964) and the University of Virginia (MA 1965). After a stint as a college teacher, he moved to the Maine coast and eventually to New York City, where he worked as a freelance writer, editor and translator, and also as a cabinet-maker. He has published two collections of poetry, many essays and reviews, and some thirty books translated from French, Italian and Russian.

LARISSA VOLOKHONSKY was born in Leningrad, attended Leningrad State University and, on graduating, joined a scientific team whose work took her to the far east of Russia, to Kamchatka and Sakhalin Island. She emigrated to Israel in 1973, and to the United States in 1975, where she attended Yale Divinity School and St. Vladimir's Theological Seminary. Soon after settling in New York City, she married Richard Pevear, and a few years later they moved to France with their two children.

Together, Pevear and Volokhonsky have translated twenty books from the Russian, including works by Fyodor Dostoevsky, Leo Tolstoy, Mikhail Bulgakov, Anton Chekhov, Boris Pasternak and Nikolai Leskov. Their translation of Dostoevsky's *The Brothers Karamazov* received the PEN Translation Prize for 1991; their translation of Tolstoy's *Anna Karenina* was awarded the same prize in 2002; and in 2006 they were awarded the first Efim Etkind International Translation Prize by the European University of St. Petersburg.